W0259582

ISBN: 9781407713502

Published by:
HardPress Publishing
8345 NW 66TH ST #2561
MIAMI FL 33166-2626

Email: info@hardpress.net
Web: http://www.hardpress.net

Cotton Growing in India

Report by
ARNO SCHMIDT,
Secretary of the
International Federation of Master Cotton Spinners' and Manufacturers' Associations

International Federation of Master Cotton Spinners' and Manufacturers' Associations

COTTON GROWING

IN

INDIA

Report by

ARNO SCHMIDT,

Secretary, on his Second Visit to India, December, 1911—January, 1912

LIST OF ILLUSTRATIONS.

INDEX.

PREFACE.

Sir Thomas W. Holderness, K.C.S.I., Secretary of the Revenue and Statistics Department of the India Office, London, referring to Mr. Schmidt's report of his first visit to India, said:—

> "I cannot do better than refer to the very admirable report of the International Federation Secretary, Mr. Arno Schmidt. I do not think I ever read a report which is a better model of what a report should be. It is thoroughly moderate, it is concise and clear, and it is the statement of fact by a man who has taken the trouble to master the question. He gives the Indian Government and its officers credit for the efforts they are making, and at the same time he is a shrewd and not unkindly critic of deficiencies which have been brought to his notice. I venture to congratulate the Federation on having such a report. I think this report will prove to be valuable and important, and will probably direct the attention of the Government to what can be done."

I venture to express the opinion that the present report of Mr. Arno Schmidt's second visit will, in view of the exhaustive information it contains, be of equal value.

Mr. Schmidt assures me that since his first visit to India a decided improvement is noticeable in many directions. The quantities of long staple cotton already produced are a confirmation of the opinion expressed by a deputation of English and Indian cotton spinners who waited upon Viscount Morley of Blackburn, O.M., then Secretary of State for India, on July 27th, 1910, that it is to India that the cotton industry must look for the speediest increase in the production of improved staple cotton.

This year about 200,000 bales of cotton, equal to Middling American, have been produced in India, and there is every reason to hope that with the increasing area under irrigation and the efficient pioneer work of the Departments of Agriculture, there will be a constant and gradual increase in the production of long staple cotton.

I recommend this Report to the careful study of Cotton Spinners and to the Colonial Cotton Growing Associations of the European Powers.

Charles W. Macara, President,
The International Federation of Master Cotton Spinners' and Manufacturers' Associations.

Manchester, May 11th, 1912.

COTTON GROWING IN INDIA.

Report of the Secretary of the International Federation of Master Cotton Spinners' and Manufacturers' Associations on his second visit to India.

December, 1911—*January,* 1912.

Introduction. Whilst the principal purpose of my first visit to India in 1909/10 was to obtain the affiliation of the Indian Millowners to the International Cotton Federation, and the secondary one to enquire into the question of Cotton Growing in that country* the terms of reference for the second Indian tour were:

> To further investigate the possibilities of Cotton Growing in India specially with a view to the study of the question of establishing Cotton Buying and Ginning Agencies in the long staple Cotton Growing districts.

My stay in India, owing to business demands at home, was limited to seven weeks, but as my visit was kindly notified by the India Office in London to the numerous officials in India connected with agriculture, I was able to arrange an almost complete itinerary of the more important cotton-growing Provinces. The information which I have collected has been communicated to me mainly by the technical agricultural experts of the Government, the Deputy Directors of Agriculture; but I also made it a point to inspect in each Province fields belonging to farmers, to question them where possible, and to elicit information from ginners and merchants.

I desire to acknowledge at the outset the great assistance rendered me by the Deputy Directors, and to emphasize the fact that during the short time that has elapsed since their appointment (these posts were only created in 1904/5) much valuable work has been accomplished.

It was only with reluctance that I ventured to give my own opinion on some of the subjects in this report, but I took the precaution to submit my views, prior to publication, to several Indian experts of many years' standing, and in most cases have my conclusions also been endorsed by the cotton millowners at Bombay and Cawnpore, where I had the time to convene meetings.

The view of an unprejudiced outsider often proves valuable, and this will, I hope, serve as a sufficient reason for opinions given, after so short a stay in the country. A fresh eye is an important factor in investigation.

During my seven weeks' travel in India, I visited Surat, Mirpukhas, Lyallpur, Gurdaspur, Aligarh, Cawnpore, Nagpur, Akola, Bombay, Dharwar, Hubli, Gadag, Madras, Virudupatti, Koil-

* Copies of the Report on the first visit can be obtained on application to the office of the International Federation.

patti, Calcutta, Cawnpore, and Bombay, a journey of 7,982 miles, and as my time was very limited I made most of the railway journeys by night.

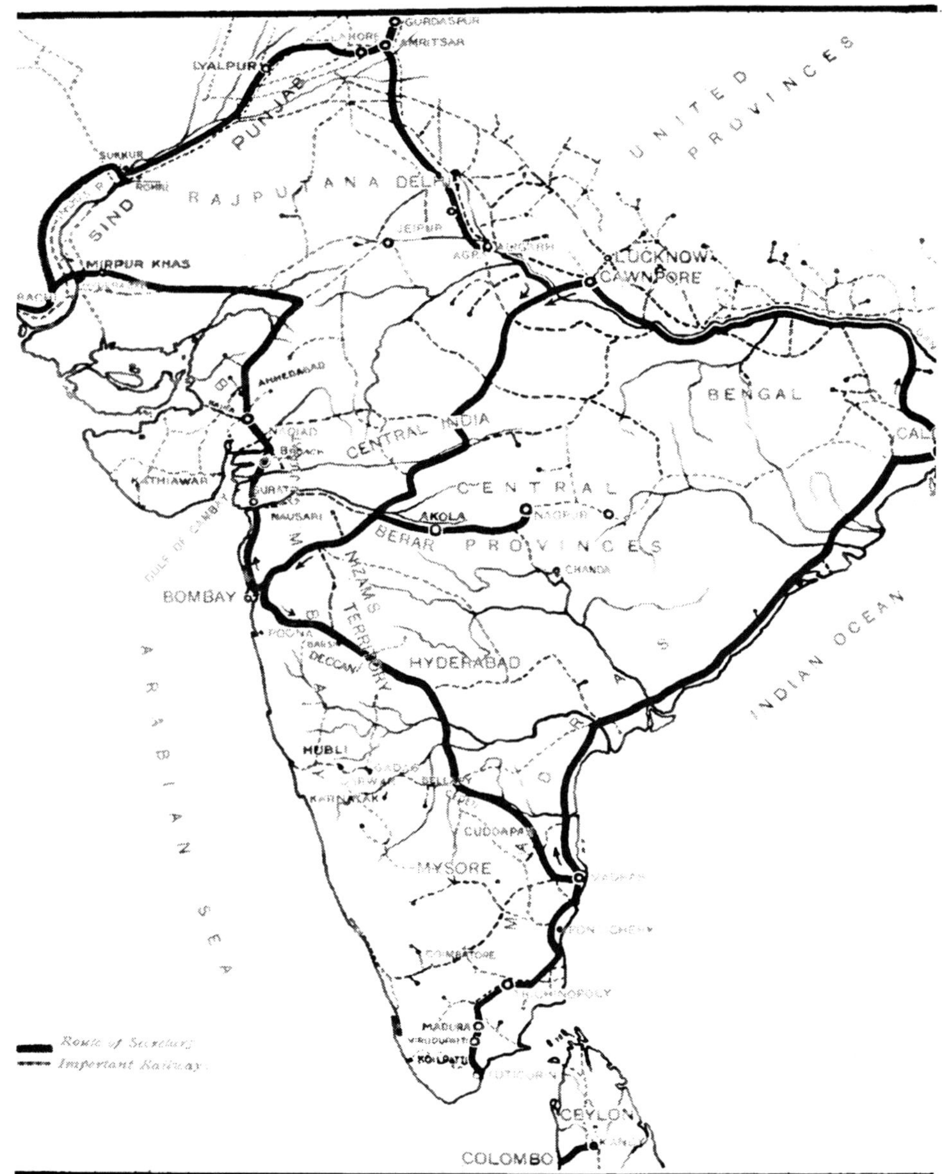

Map of India, showing Route of Secretary.

As this report is intended not only for the spinners of the world, but also for the Colonial Cotton Growing Associations of the European Powers, I have included some technical agricultural notes which might not be of direct interest to the cotton spinner. The summary and conclusions will be of more interest to the spinner.

To generalise on cotton growing in India would be unprofitable, for the climatic and soil conditions of this vast country vary perhaps more than in any other country in the world; for example, in the North of India the cotton crop is being harvested in October, whilst in the South the seed is being put into the ground at that time. Almost all the year through cotton is being picked somewhere in India. For these reasons I am compelled to treat each cotton-growing tract separately. I shall begin with a description of the conditions in the Madras Presidency, as the advent of the new kind of cotton, "Cambodia," is of far-reaching and immediate importance to the cotton spinners of the world, and to the cotton producers of India; then I shall deal with the Central Provinces, owing to the excellent system of administration existing in these parts. Bombay Presidency, the Punjab, and the United Provinces, as well as Eastern Bengal and Assam, will also be dealt with.

Finally, I shall submit the conclusions at which I have arrived as the result of my investigations.

MADRAS PRESIDENCY.

The principal Cotton Growing districts are: Madura and Tinnevelly and Coimbatore in the South of the Presidency, a portion of Kistna which abuts on the Deccan, and the Ceded districts (Bellary, Anantapur, and Cuddapah).

"Cambodia" or "Tinnevelly American."

The outstanding feature in agriculture in this district is the recent introduction of Cambodia cotton; it closely resembles American Upland, and is probably of the same species; it is one inch staple, uniform in length, glossy, somewhat creamy in appearance, and its fibre is fine, yet strong. This cotton had been detected some five years ago accidentally by Mr. A. Steele, of Messrs. A. & F. Harvey & Co., at their gin in Virudupatti. I am told that the merit of introducing and spreading this cotton over the South of India is to a very large extent due to Mr. Steele.

When Cambodia cotton, which is known in Liverpool as "Tinnevelly American," was first detected, it had a ginning outturn of 44 per cent. (44lbs. fibre in 100lbs. seed cotton), but it fell quickly to 33 per cent. This percentage has been maintained during the last few years, and it is anticipated that it will be increased again by more careful cultivation. Cambodia is the name given to this cotton by the Agricultural Department, which traces its origin to Indo-China, but no doubt it came originally from the United States. Mr. H. Sampson, Deputy Director of Agriculture, Southern Division, Madras, writes about this cotton in the "Agricultural Journal of India," Volume IV., Part 4, as follows:—

"The introduction of Cambodia cotton into the Madras Presidency is perhaps one of the most striking instances in India of how readily the ryot will take up a new cultivation, if once he is satisfied that it pays him to do so. In this case it is still more remarkable because cotton is no new crop to the ryot, and the cultivation of this Cambodia cotton is very different to the methods of cotton cultivation known for generations to the ryots of the Southern Districts. The indigenous cotton has always been essentially a rain-fed crop of the black cotton soil. This, in the dry climate of the south, cannot stand heavy manuring, which tends to keep the root system near the surface. Cambodia cotton, however, if it is to pay, has to be grown as an irrigated crop on heavily-manured soil, and if anyone had five years ago told the ryots of Tinnevelly, Ramnad and Madura that in five years' time their best garden lands (*i.e.*, heavily-manured made soils under well irrigation) would be sown with cotton as an irrigated crop, the very idea would have been laughed to scorn. Yet this is what has happened even to the ousting of such profitable crops as chillies and tobacco.

"It is, however, in this climate, much hardier and more vigorous, and gives a stronger and fuller lint than either newly-introduced American or acclimatised Dharwar American. Its root system closely resembles that of American Upland, viz., a tapering tap-root with strong feeding roots given off near the surface, and differs greatly from that of the indigenous cottons which have a long, slender tap-root with very slender feeding roots penetrating deeply into the soil. It can be understood, therefore, why it is that Cambodia responds so readily to irrigation, and how, since the crop is protected from drought, it is possible to manure heavily and obtain very heavy yields, and it can also be understood why this crop, if grown on black cotton soil with the aid of rain alone, cannot resist prolonged drought. On well-manured land under irrigation the yield is usually stated to be from 1,250lbs. to 1,600lbs. of Kappas (seed cotton) and never less; while yields as high as 2,500lbs. have been reported. With a ginning percentage of 33 to 35 per cent. of lint, an acre will, at this rate, give about a bale of lint (500lbs.) or over."

In 1907-8 the crop amounted in all to 40 bales of 500lbs., and the seed obtained from it was eagerly sought for. In 1909 the crop was 1,650 bales, in 1910 7,500 bales, last year it was 30,000 bales, and this year, it is estimated, the crop will be at least 80,000 bales of 500lbs. (It must be noted that the Indian bales coming from the South weigh 500lbs., whilst the usual Indian bale only weighs 400lbs.)

Cambodia must not be grown too near rice fields, as the large quantity of water necessary for rice cultivation makes impossible the prevention of the saturation of the adjoining Cambodia fields and the bringing up of salt.

In view of the recent developments with regard to the purchase of cotton plantations in the United States of America and Africa by cotton spinning firms in Europe, I made enquiries as to whether the Government would welcome European spinners in acquiring land in districts newly developed for irrigation. Anglo-Indians told me that such a step would probably not be welcomed by the Government, and on enquiry at the Department of Revenue and Agriculture in India I was informed that "if any definite proposals were laid before the Government they would receive careful consideration.'' In this connection I may mention that one native gentleman offered me 1,000 acres of cotton-growing land in one of the Native States in the South of India, situated about six miles from the railway. He has himself leased the land from a native chief on the following terms :—

2 rupees assessment per acre per annum for 6 years, and
6 ,, ,, ,, for each succeeding year.

The lease is only for 30 years. The land can be acquired on a permanent ownership at the price of 6 rupees per year. I was told that 20,000 acres, which, however, are not yet growing cotton, could be obtained at a yearly payment of 6 rupees per acre on permanent ownership. The transfer fees and preliminary expenses (which would entail no doubt a number of baksheesh) are estimated at 3 rupees per acre.

This quick increase in the production shows how eagerly the people have taken up the cultivation of cotton. Everywhere in the South one can notice wells being bored simply for the purpose of being able to grow this cotton. Cambodia has replaced such crops as chilli, tobacco and rice (on poor land). It requires only two or three irrigations in addition to the usual 27-30 inch rainfall. The cost of construction of a well sufficient for supplying the water for two acres is about 300-500 rupees. An advantage in connection with the cultivation of this cotton is that it does not encroach upon the land devoted to the ordinary Tinnevelly cotton. Cambodia can be grown only in red soil, whilst the Tinnevelly flourishes in black soil; thus the crop of the latter will this year be again 90,000 bales. The average yield of Cambodia cotton is 500lbs. of lint per acre, an extraordinary yield, if one remembers that cotton in India does not yield more than 90lbs. to 100lbs. on an average.

The Cambodia seed being covered with many linters it is necessary to roll it in cow dung in order that, whilst sowing, the seeds may not stick together. Sowing generally takes place in October; broadcast sowing is practically the only method. Prior to the sowing the soil is ploughed twice or three times by means of the ordinary wooden native plough. Ten pounds of seed are required for one acre; two or three times the field is weeded by hand. Two or three waterings are required during the growing season, and the water is obtained by means of primitive lifting machines. Picking begins in the middle of February, and is carried on every alternate day. The pickers, who are mostly women, are exceedingly careful in their work. This is quite contrary to what is generally the custom in India. Cotton in the South of India is only picked early in the morning, when the dew is on the plants, and this is done in order that no dry leaves or other impurities may be mixed with the cotton. Picking ceases at 10 a.m., as by that time the temperature is very high, and the plants get dry and brittle. In order that the cotton may not retain any excessive moisture, it is the general custom of the cultivators to spread the picked cotton along the side of the field and expose it to the sun.

The cultivator is described as a hard working and intelligent man; it is, however, interesting to note how suspicious he is of Government action. The Government endeavoured to find out the area that is grown under Cambodia, and many farmers, fearing that Government wanted to levy a special tax on this remunerative crop, pulled up the Cambodia plants.

The *ginneries* are all in the hands of well-known European firms. Cambodia requires a slower ginning process than the ordinary Tinnevelly. So far only roller gins are used, and I was told that the Saw gins, such as are used in America and also in Dharwar, south of the Bombay Presidency, would cause too much damage to the fibre. Whilst the rollers of the gin for Tinnevelly cotton are run at a speed of 1,000 revolutions per minute, they must not go faster than 750 revolutions per minute for Cambodia. This accounts for the difference in price in the cost of ginning, Tinnevelly being charged at 5 rupees per 500lbs., whilst Cambodia pays 5 rupees 8 annas, including baling. Cambodia seed, being bigger and more fluffy than Tinnevelly, requires a broader grid in the gin. I may remark here that for this reason it will be an easy matter to keep the seed of the two kinds of cotton apart in the ginneries. The gins begin working in the middle of February and do not finish until Christmas. From April to September two shifts of 12 hours each are working. The wages for women at the gin are 4 annas per day, for men performing light work 8 annas, for those performing hard work 12 annas.

There are only two grades of Cambodia cotton, the first being from the pickings which take place from February to April; the cotton from these is by far the better. The second grade is that represented by the second picking, which is obtained after the summer rains in May. This second picking is generally called the "second flush"; when the first picking is finished and the plants do not look as though they would yield any more, it is usually the time when heavy thunder rains fall in Southern India, and these put new life into the plants. Within a very short time after the rains fresh bloom appears, and finally the bolls form and mature. This "second flush" gives a smaller yield, and is inferior in quality. I was assured that the grade of Cambodia all over the south of India does not vary very much; this is different from Tinnevelly, of which there exist some eight different grades.

Cambodia cotton is highly appreciated by the cotton spinners in the south of India; in the north it is hardly known yet, as the cost of transportation from the south to the north is almost as heavy as that of shipping the cotton to Europe. One spinner told me that he uses this cotton for 40's, another stated that he produced with this cotton alone a very good 30's twist, and that he improved his low Middling American with it. I have seen beautiful linings and white shirtings produced from yarn made entirely of this cotton. Some of the spinning mills in the south have recently put up new machinery in order to use with advantage this long staple cotton. Indian cotton manufacturers have opened up a new market for fine goods, which until the discovery of Cambodia cotton they could not produce economically. One of the spinning firms had an advertisement in the Madras local papers with a view to stimulating the cultivation of this Cambodia cotton round Madras City, giving particulars of how the cotton is to be grown. The difference between the price of the ordinary local cotton and Cambodia is 1d. per pound. Most of the Cambodia crop last year was sent to various parts of Europe.

In discussing the future of this Cambodia cotton I was told that we might in 10 years' time have easily one million bales of Cambodia grown in the south of India, and these should replace an equal number of bales of American cotton. The great necessity for a rational and sound expansion of this wonderful Cambodia seems to centre, in my opinion, *in the immediate establishment of Seed Farms, which should devote half of their land every year to growing this cotton alone.* The fact that the ginning out-turn has come down from 44 to 33 per cent. is a proof of either wrong cultivation or of the mixing of the seed with other kinds. On one occasion I debated, with three experts, the question of Seed Farms for the exclusive purpose of growing Cambodia, and they agreed with me that the only way to improve the ginning out-turn and to keep the characteristics of Cambodia pure would be for the Government to start at once a Seed Farm of, say, 400 acres, and to devote every year 200 acres of it solely to the growing of pure Cambodia. The cotton crop on the Seed Farm would pay well for the expenditure, and would enable the Government to sell pure seed at a very cheap rate. Such a Seed Farm would be a paying concern from the outset, and its benefits would be :—

(*a*) The obtaining and distributing of pure seed.
(*b*) The demonstration of proper cultivation.
(*c*) A financial gain.

The farm should be situated in the vicinity of Trichinopoly, and in order to prevent self-hybridisation no other cotton should be grown on this 200 acres.

I was assured that bribes are often given when native subalterns are entrusted with the disposal of seed. Although from personal experience I can hardly credit the statement made to me by many Anglo-Indians, I think it will be well if a sharp eye on those who are engaged in the selling of the seed and produce of the Government farms is kept.

In speaking about bribery amongst the Native Government Officials, I may here relate evidence which I have received not only from Government Officials, but also from farmers in two Provinces.

The Indian Government frequently makes advances for the purpose of assisting farmers in the purchase of seed or agricultural machinery; such advances are known under the name of "Takavi." A small rate of interest in charged (6 per cent. per annum) and the money is encashed by easy instalments through the Revenue Department. There accrues hardly any loss to the Government from these advances, as the cultivators refund the loan honourably. When I spoke in the Bombay Presidency of the comparatively little use to which this "Takavi" is put by farmers, I was told that in the first instance there is so much "red tape" to be gone through that many months elapse before the loan is handed over, and that it consequently comes too late. Whilst one can understand a delay in the granting of the loans, it is unpardonable that comparatively a large amount of the advances made is paid in commissions and bribes to Native Government Officials, thus mitigating the advantage of a small rate of interest. One of the Commissioners, in one of the official speeches he made, deplored this state of affairs, and as the statement came from such a high official I must reluctantly accept it as correct.

A Seed Farm ought to possess its own gin, worked by an oil engine such as is used largely in the Central Provinces. (*See* remarks under Central Provinces, p. 23).

Ginneries. The exporters of Southern India, who are at the same time the ginners, buy the cotton only after they have ginned it. This is different from the practice in vogue in the other Provinces. Most of the spinning mills have their own gins attached to the mill. I was told by several ginners that the present rate of ginning and pressing, say, 5-6 rupees per 500lbs. ginned cotton, does not pay them.

Hand ginning, which until three years ago was much in use, has now died out completely; Platts' roller gins only are in use.

As stated above, the bales of Southern Madras are of 500lbs. weight. They are pressed as follows :—

40 cubic feet per ton for Indian mills.
44 ,, ,, ,, Japanese Mills.
50 ,, ,, ,, European Mills.

The Japanese spinners maintain that the pressure necessary for obtaining 50 cubic feet injures the fibre. One double roller gin turns out per 12 hours about 1,000lbs. Cambodia cotton, whilst in Egypt the gins turn out in the same period 1,320lbs., therefore some improvement in the Indian gins should be possible.

The exporters whom I consulted told me that their margin of profit did not on an average exceed one rupee per bale, and that the Japanese spinners, who had established a Buying Agency in this district a few years ago soon found out that it did not pay them to maintain it. There is very keen competition for all the cotton grown in the South of India, and consequently there is no need for a Buying Agency.

One of the deputy directors expressed the opinion that the piling up of cotton prior to ginning, as shown in the following illustration, must be injurious, as it heats the seed and consequently spoils its germinating power. Other experts expressed themselves as opposed to this view.

Tinnevelly Cotton. "Tinnevelly Cotton" is grown chiefly on the black cotton soil plains found in the Northern parts of Tinnevelly and the Southern parts of Madura, but with the produce of these tracts some of the produce of Tanjore, Trichinopoly, Coimbatore, and Salem is exported under the same name. It is one of the most highly-prized of Indian cottons and one of the few which are suitable for mixing with "American"; it commands from 1d. to $\frac{3}{4}$d. per pound lower price than Mid-American It is valued chiefly for its colour, which is very white; it also excels in cleanness and freedom from leaf and in strength of fibre. The fibre is not particularly long. Tinnevelly cotton usually comes into the market in good condition, but adulteration with seed cotton, sand, and other foreign matters is practised.

Westerns.

As I did not pay a visit to the northern part of the Kistna district, although some is also raised from a Government report: "Westerns may, according to the Madras Chamber of Commerce, be divided into 'Westerns' and 'Northerns,' the former coming from the

Stacks of Seed-Cotton in the yard of a Ginning Factory.

country north of Bellary and Kurnool, the latter from those parts of Cuddapah and Kurnool lying in the Nandyal valley and some portion of Anantapur about Tadpatri. Apparently the mixing of the two classes is a source of complaint, the former being inferior to the latter, which, though not so white, is more silky. 'Westerns' proper from Kurnool, Bellary, and the Nizam's dominions is longer stapled than 'Tinnevelly,' and the colour is fairly white, but it is dull, rough, and often mixed with broken leaf and seed. Its value is about $\frac{1}{2}$d. a pound less than Tinnevelly, and it is frequently adulterated with seed, but the presence of large quantities of seed in this class of cotton is often attributable to the practice, specially adopted in the Nizam's dominions, of cleaning it by foot-rollers.

Northerns.

"'Northerns' are silkier than 'Westerns,' and, were it not for the slightly red tinge they have, would be in more demand than they are. They, however, command from $\frac{1}{8}$d. to $\frac{3}{16}$d. per pound more than 'Westerns,' with which they are often mixed. This variation in the colour of the lint appears to be due to the nature of the soil on which the crop has been grown; that produced on 'Regada' (black cotton soil) being superior in colour and fineness, whilst that produced on the red and mixed soils is not nearly so white and is of inferior quality. Even on the black soils different varieties produce samples of different character and value. There appears to have been a gradual improvement in the condition of the cotton brought to market in recent years, probably owing to more careful preparation. In the localities where these cottons are grown, several experiments have been made with other varieties, viz., Broach, Bourbon, New Orleans, and Nankin. The second and last-named varieties have not succeeded. The first-named crop succeeded during the first year in which it was tried, but it appears to require a heavier rainfall than is met with in Bellary and earlier sowing than is there practised. The New Orleans variety grows freely in Kurnool, but the difficulty of separating the seed from the lint makes the ryots unwilling to grow it as a crop.

Cocanadas.

"'Cocanadas' is produced chiefly in the Kistna district, although some is also raised in the Godavari, but the latter is chiefly consumed locally. This class of cotton occupies a position in the estimation of the English market between 'Tinnevelly' and 'Westerns,' being worth about $\frac{1}{2}$d. less than the former and from $\frac{1}{4}$d. to $\frac{1}{2}$d. more than the latter. The staple is of moderate length and strength and silky, but has a red tinge; it is valued by the manufacturers of coloured yarns, and is used also in the manufacture of lace. The redness of this class of cotton is peculiar, and the best qualities come from the Palnad taluk of the Kistna, whilst that from other localities is very varied."

Government Seed Farms.

The Government has about 50 seed farms, of an average area of eight acres, distributed all over the Presidency. These farms are owned by cultivators, but the Department of Agriculture supervises the cultivation and buys the seed cotton back, gins it, and distributes the seed. A premium of four rupees per 500lbs. seed cotton is paid by the Government for cotton grown on these seed farms, but the stipulation is made that the cotton must be perfectly dry. The owners of the seed farms have to sign an agreement that the cotton is to be sold back to the Government and that they will cultivate the cotton in drills instead of broadcast sowing, which is the general custom in the southern part of Madras presidency. In this manner the Department of Agriculture obtains annually seed sufficient to supply 12,000-15,000 acres; it has opened up some 70 seed depôts in various villages. These depôts are a necessity, because just before the sowing season, journeys of long distances by road are impracticable owing to the heavy rains.

There are some Agricultural Associations in Madras, but so far they have not been of much practical use. The Co-operative Credit Societies are beginning to make themselves felt.

Fraudulent Damping of Cotton.

As regards artificial damping, I was told that the farmers do not as a rule resort to this practice in the southern part, but Western cottons in the north are mixed frequently with salpetre, which takes up readily the moisture of the atmosphere.

There is no scarcity of labour in the South of India.

The wages for picking cotton are mostly paid in kind, the pickers receiving from one-sixteenth to one-quarter of the cotton picked, according to the variety.

As regards insects, there is not much cause for complaint in the South of India; besides small quantities of aphis there exist cotton insects only at Erode, where perennial cotton is grown.

Necessity for increasing the staff.

One of the deputy directors told me that although he had already been in this district for seven years, he had not yet been able to visit all the districts which are likely to grow cotton. As the particular deputy director is a most zealous and energetic man, this circumstance proves clearly the absolute necessity for an additional European deputy director for this province. Most of the Anglo-Indians agree that, although in future years the higher posts in the Department of Agriculture might be thrown open to Indian gentlemen, still, as long as there is a great deal of pioneer work to be done, these higher posts should be filled by Europeans with University training and practical experience in farming.

Cultivation.

Whilst in the northern part of the Madras Presidency all the cotton is sown in drills, in the south only broadcast sowing is resorted to. In the north several kinds of crops are planted in one field all mixed together. This is done in order that at all events some crop may be raised. One can notice, for instance, Jowari (a kind of millet) mixed with cotton, and when one approaches such a field one can at first sight only recognise the crop which stands highest, viz., Jowari. It is claimed that this method is advantageous for the farmer in districts where the rain is uncertain, as in the north. Where these mixed crops of cotton and cereals are planted there is no need for any rotation of crops, but in the south it is the custom to plant two years consecutively cereals and the next year cotton.

Manure is applied only to the cereals. In the black cotton soil district of Coimbatore no rotation of crops is practised. Thinning out in dry districts where rains are uncertain is not considered advisable, because the plants in consequence of the thinning out branch out and grow too vigorously, so much indeed that during the time of the maturing period, when the plants require a great amount of moisture, they suffer considerably, as the available moisture cannot feed the vigorous plants.

The system of manuring adopted by good farmers in this Presidency is to allow about a thousand sheep to graze on one acre during one night. The farmers have to pay for this about 4 rupees per night. Generally this is done only by the best farmers; the ordinary ryot does not manure his cotton soil as a rule, but considers it sufficient for cotton to receive the residue of manure which has been applied to the preceding crop. A very interesting experiment as to the value of manuring was brought to my notice at the Koilpatti

THE CAWNPORE CHAIN-PUMP.

It can be worked by hand, bullock, or oil-engine; it is claimed that it lifts water from a 30 feet depth.

Government farm, where one acre, treated with cattle manure mixed with urine, produced 1,000lbs. seed cotton of Tinnevelly, against 300lbs. in unmanured ground.

As regards the wells which are in use in many parts of India, and that are being bored in the South of Madras, I am inclined to think that they might be considerably improved. The Cawnpore chain-pump (illustration above) and some of the Egyptian water-wheels could in many cases be used with greater efficiency. Care should be taken that all machinery at the Government Agricultural farms should be kept in perfect condition, and that, for instance, the buckets used at the wells should not leak. I have seen a good many defective buckets used in connection with these draw-wells, and the accompanying illustration shows the great amount of waste of water occasioned through leakage of the bucket; the photo was taken on a Government farm.

A Leaking Bucket on a Demonstration Farm.

Land Values. These have increased considerably in the Madras Presidency during the last few years; recently a farmer in the south paid for purely agricultural land 1,000 rupees for 3¾ acres. The annual land assessment is 2 rupees per acre. Where rice is grown a charge of 10 rupees per acre for irrigation water is levied, but where there are wells, *i.e.*, in all the districts where Cambodia is grown, there is no charge for irrigation, as the wells are made by the cultivators.

CENTRAL PROVINCES AND BERAR.

I may be excused for giving detailed information as regards cotton growing in the Central Provinces, as judging from what I have seen on my visits to the various districts, I consider that the administration and the practical management of the Agricultural Department of the Central Provinces may be considered the most perfect in the whole of India. This is largely due to the expert knowledge which the Director of Agriculture, Mr. C. E. Law, C.I.E., has obtained through his many years of service and through the able manner in which he is being assisted by his Deputy Directors, who are working with him in a most harmonious manner. I may here mention that the posts of Directors of Agriculture are filled from the Indian Civil Service, and that these gentlemen are intended to act principally in an administrative manner. The technical experts are the *Deputy* Directors, who have had a specialised university training in agriculture and practical experience in farming. During the last few years two of the *Directors* have studied agriculture in England.

The Central Provinces and Berar are the second largest cotton-growing district of India, the area under cultivation being this year 4,500,000 acres. It is interesting to note that in 1868 only two million acres were grown under cotton in this tract. The geographical position of the cotton tract is Berar, Nimar, Nagpur, Wardha, and on a small scale throughout the Provinces.

The crop of the last season being much higher than the previous one, it is estimated that 320lbs. of seed cotton per acre would be a fair average, and the amount of lint is 35 per cent. The rains began on the 12th June, and with the first break of the monsoon from 3 to 10 inches fell. Many cultivators had sown their fields after the first break of the monsoon, but as there was an interval of three weeks before the second rains came, many young plants were damaged through the drought, and a large part of the area required replanting; therefore the crop was about three weeks later than usual. Notwithstanding this short drought the crop has been a good one.

The kinds of cotton grown are:—

KINDS OF COTTON.

Variety.	App. Staple.	Average Yield for 4 Years in lbs. per acre.			Value at this year's Prices in Nagpur C. P.	
	Inch.	of Kapas (seed-cotton).	of Lint.	of Seed.	Rs.	As.
G. Malvensis	7/8	373	112	261	57	5
G. Vera	3/4	343	115	228	51	11
G. rosea	almost 5/8	402	161	241	69	14
G. rosea cutchica ..	1/2	412	150	262	66	0
Berar Jari	5/8 (mixture different	371 of 65 varieties)	132	239	58	5
Buri (G. hirsutum) ..	1	303	100	203	57	15
Bani (G. indicum) ..	1	255	74	181	44	3

Buri is now only grown on the rich village lands and in those districts where cotton is generally affected by wilt. Buri is entirely immune from this disease. About 600,000 acres of this cotton are grown, which produce 1,500 bales. These have been bought every year by a Nagpur spinning mill.

Bani is a silky, fine cotton, of 1in. staple, perhaps the finest cotton grown in India. It was largely exported at one time under the name of "Hinganghats," but the yield per acre is about one-quarter less than that of the local Jari, and the ginning out-turn is only 26 per cent. for Bani against 35 per cent. for Jari. Taking the yield per acre and the ginning out-turn into consideration, the advantages for the grower are considerably in favour of Jari cotton, and consequently Bani has practically been given up. The ginner fixes his value almost entirely on the ginning out-turn, and consequently the cultivator receives less money per pound of seed cotton of Bani than per pound of seed cotton of Jari.

Bani is grown mixed with Jari in the Nizam's Territory, and in small parts of the borderland of Berar adjoining the former. There is certainly no *pure* Bani grown anywhere except on the Government experimental farms.

Mr. D. Clouston, one of the Deputy Directors of Agriculture, writes in the "Agricultural Journal of India" about these cottons as follows :—

"It is certain that large quantities of such long-stapled cottons as *Bani* and *Buri*, which Lancashire requires, could be grown in the Central Provinces and Berar should the prices paid for the lint prove remunerative to the grower. At present they do not, except under the very special conditions to be noted later. It will be gathered from the statement below that, if we were to deal directly with Lancashire instead of disposing of the lint locally, the price realised for our short-stapled cotton, relative to that of middling American, would be even higher than the trade pays for it here, and that to substitute a long-stapled cotton for it would, under these circumstances, prove still less remunerative for the cultivator. By exporting his cotton to Lancashire he would, under the most favourable conditions, get about 33 per cent. more for a long-stapled cotton such as Bani, than for his short-stapled Rosea; but the out-turn of lint of the latter would, on the other hand, exceed that of the former by about 117 per cent., so that, if he were to grow and export Bani at present prices, it would be at a comparatively heavy loss."

Variety.	Valuation of Lint per lb., in December, 1910, by			Middling American.
	Manager, Empress Mills, Nagpur.	Wolstenholme and Holland, Liverpool.	Gaddum & Co., Manchester.	
Rosea ..	6·49d.	7d.	6·75d.	—
Malvensis ..	7·42d.	8·20d.	7·75d.—8d.	
Buri ..	8·67d.	7·90d.—8d.	8d.—8·25d.	8·07d.
Bani ..	8·81d.	8·40d.	8d.—8·25d.	

"*Rosea* is a hardy variety and therefore suffers less than others from the vicissitudes of the climate and the cracking of the black cotton soil in the Central Provinces and

Berar; it is the earliest, too, of all the races grown, and its seed gives the highest germinating percentage. It is capable of great improvement in its ginning percentage by plant-to-plant selection. The selection strain which is now being propagated on the Seed Farms has given an average of 40·3 per cent. of lint. If it were possible to substitute rosea for the kind now grown, the higher ginning percentage alone would in a normal year result in an increase in the Central Provinces and Berar of 51,000,000lbs. of lint. The Agricultural experts believe that this is possible and that to effect it merely requires time and organisation, as the cultivators everywhere are clamouring for the seed.

Rosea cutchica is slightly inferior in the quality of its staple to rosea and gives from 2 to 3 per cent. less lint.

Malvensis and *vera* give about the same out-turn of lint, which is nearly equal in quality to that of bani. There is great variation in the quality and percentage of lint of different strains of malvensis, and it is therefore believed that there is much scope for that reason for its further improvement."

I inspected various fields belonging to cultivators; most of them were tolerably well tilled, all the cotton was sown in lines on the flat. In examining the cotton I found clearly six different kinds growing in one field, all mixed, rosea, rosea cutchica, vera, malvensis, bani, and Georgian cotton, *i.e.*, cotton varying from half-inch to one inch staple and varying largely in yield and ginning out-turn. This mixture is commonly known as *Berar Jari*.

Water Supply.

There is no irrigation required in this district for the growing of cotton. The crop in this province depends entirely upon rain; irrigation is only required for the cultivation of rice in the north of the province, in Chhattasgarh and Chanda. In these irrigated tracts experiments are now being carried on with Cambodia and Buri cottons, and it will depend on the success of these whether an opening for these cottons will be made; there will be, owing to new irrigation works, some two million acres at disposal. Short stapled cotton is grown in these districts on a limited scale, but with the introduction of irrigation it is anticipated that long stapled cotton will flourish. During the time of the American Civil War these tracts grew considerable quantities of cotton.

Land Tenure.

In the Central Provinces the villages are held by landowners whose proprietorship is clearly recognised, though their rights of ownership are subject to the rights of occupancy of their tenants. Both proprietor and tenant are given security of tenure in the land, with the object of encouraging each to make the best possible use of it. This system has produced a number of village proprietors who often cultivate large home-farms, intelligent farmers, who are willing to test improved methods and to lay out substantial capital sums, if they are convinced that an adequate return is likely to be secured. Amongst the tenantry there is also a sprinkling of men who cultivate large holdings and employ large capital; and such men are even more numerous in the rich province of Berar, where the "ryotwari system" of tenure prevails. The difficulties in introducing improvements are, therefore, not so great as in a tract where the land is parcelled out into minute holdings and where the capital at the disposal of each holder is extremely limited, for there are numbers of cultivators ready to expend some hundreds of rupees upon a new implement, an improved method of cultivation, or the like, provided they are convinced that the outlay will give a substantial return. The standard of farming attained in different parts of these provinces varies considerably, but it is on the whole inferior to that of most other parts of India, so that there is much more scope for improvement than in provinces where cultivation has already a high level. In the Central Provinces, as a rule, land is plentiful and intensive cultivation is but little practised; in Berar, on the other hand, the great boom in the cotton trade has enormously increased the demand for land, with the result that grazing areas have been curtailed and the standard of cultivation has reached a much higher level. Good cultivators are found as exceptions among all the different castes, but the best cultivators are the hereditary cultivating castes.

In each district there is an active *Agricultural Association* of which the Deputy-Commissioner is the President. The members of these associations are the leading landholders, and a spirit of mutual respect and co-operation is being fostered by these associations. Discussions on new methods of cultivation, demonstrations, exchange of experience gained, &c., occupy the attention of the members at their meetings. It is recognised as a great honour for a man to belong to an agricultural association in the Central Provinces. These associations also promote loyalty, and are an excellent means for the Department of Agriculture to distribute the results obtained by their experiments. These associations are also organising pig-sticking hunts, as the crops suffer considerably from wild boars. The Seed Farms are owned by some of the members of these agricultural associations.

Seed Farms.

Perhaps the most important organisation for the improvement of the quality in the Central Provinces is the Seed Farm. The Government possesses two central Government Farms, from which selected seed is supplied every year; in fact, the progress of Cotton Growing in the Central Provinces and Berar must be attributed mainly to the excellent organisation and management of these Seed Farms. In no other province are Seed Farms as numerous; 42 farms had been established during 1911, and the number will be increased. It is anticipated that there will be some 60 Seed Farms in working order in 1912, but here again the limit will be reached next year, unless the Government will engage an additional European Deputy Director, as the Seed Farms cannot extend sufficiently for want of suitable supervision. It would certainly be a great pity to hamper an extension of this useful work, which is highly appreciated by the cultivators, as well as by the spinners, for the sake of some £600 to £800 salary a year, and I am told that this salary has already been provided for in the Budget. The Government Agricultural farms in the Central Provinces are now self-supporting, which is an important factor.

The method of establishing and working these Seed Farms is the following: Leading landholders, who are also members of the agricultural associations, were in the first instance selected by the Director of Agriculture as suitable men to look after the Seed Farm, and for one year or two the Government guaranteed to these men to make up any loss resulting from the introduction of the improved methods of cultivation which the Department recommended in working the farm. As a matter of fact, in no single case has a loss been sustained, and there is now a distinct demand from the cultivators themselves for an extension of this system of Seed Farms. At first selected seed was supplied to the owner of the farm free of cost and the Department undertook to look after the sale of seed produced; now the owners of the Seed Farms are paying 2½ times the price ruling in the Bazaar for selected seed, and they themselves arrange for the sale and distribution of the seed at as much as three times the price of ordinary cotton seed. The Agricultural Department supervises solely the cultivation and ginning and advertises the seed in its monthly vernacular periodical, which has a circulation of over 6,000 copies. The chief difficulty experienced up to now has been that of getting the seed ginned at the proper time and of preventing the mixture of various kinds during the time of ginning. At the commencement of the movement all the ginning of the seed grown on these special farms was done by hand gins (churkhas, see illustration); their capacity is of course very limited, as only 25lbs. of seed cotton can be worked in one day with one of these implements. Several owners of Seed Farms have now decided to purchase an oil engine and two or three gins; the oil engine will be used not only for driving the gin, but for other purposes such as pumping water, chopping cattle food, &c. The Government has advanced the money necessary for this machinery out of the Takavi loans,

The particulars of the ginning plant ordered for these Seed Farms are as follows:—

	Rupees.
"Gardener" Oil Engine of 6 h.p.	1,200
Two Roller Gins	560
Cost of shed	240
so that with a capital outlay of	Rs. 2,000

each Seed Farm will be able to gin its own cotton and some of that of the neighbouring farmers. On the supposition that each of these gins will be able to handle 525lbs. lint per day, and this is certainly possible, the net cost calculated will be as follows:—

	Rupees.
Interest at 6 per cent. per annum on Rs. 2,000	120
Kerosine Oil	225
Lubricating Oil	22
Wages, Engineman and four Coolies	112
Depreciation and Repairs	250
Annual Working Expenses	Rs. 729

In three months the gins ought to deliver at least 47·250lbs. lint, therefore the cost of ginning works out to Rs.4.5.0. per 280lbs., whilst the average cost of ginning at an Akola gin is Rs.3.8.0. (sometimes 4 rupees) per 280lbs. lint, therefore causing an apparent loss of 13 annas per 280lbs., but if we consider that the oil engine will be used for other purposes as well and that the seed will have three times the value of the ordinary seed, it will clearly be an advantage to the owners of these Seed Farms to invest in these plants.

134,464lbs. improved cotton seed of rosea, buri, and malvensis were distributed through the 22 Seed Farms in 1910, and the number being now (1911) 42, about twice as much seed will have been distributed (10lbs. seed are required for one acre). As far as is practicable, entire villages are kept to one and the same strain of selected cotton. These 42 Seed Farms are supplied every year with absolutely pure seed from one of the two central Seed Farms which are under the direct supervision of the Deputy Director of Agriculture. I inspected one of these central Seed Farms for the Central Provinces and Berar, viz., that which is situated at Akola. The farm has about 245 acres under cultivation, out of these 210 are under cotton and 35 are under "jowar," which serves principally for the feeding of cattle on the farm; at the same time selected strains of pure Jowar seed are produced. Each of the varieties of cotton contained in the Berar Jari has been carefully separated and is grown on *large* areas absolutely pure. When the owner of the seed farm receives seed from the central or "nucleus" farm, he gives an undertaking that he will grow the seed on the lines laid down by the Department of Agriculture; he undertakes, for instance, to manure the field, to gin the cotton raised separately, and to use it either himself or sell it to others for sowing and not for feeding or crushing purposes. The Department has constantly applications for new seed by cultivators who are willing not only to pay a high price for the selected seed, but also to accept the conditions above referred to, and this is a sure sign that the work of the Department is fully appreciated and that there is an undoubted improvement in quality and an increase in quantity taking place every year. The Akola Seed Farm produces twice as much cotton per acre as the average farm in the Central Provinces, and this is merely due to a more intensive cultivation carried on at the farm. In order to ensure that the seed is being kept pure a small ginnery, containing two Platts' roller gins worked by a portable 5 h.p. steam engine of Marshall, Sons, & Co., Gainsborough, has been installed. The cost of the shed, engines and gins is about 5,000 rupees, and providing for all expenses, interest on capital and depreciation, as well as labour, the cost of ginning comes to almost 6 rupees per 280lbs.; 525lbs. lint are ginned every day during the three months season.

The whole farm, in consequence of its sound management, does not only act as a "nucleus" for the other seed farms and as a demonstration to the many farmers who visit it, but it also realises a very handsome profit. I cannot recommend the farm too highly as an example well worth emulation in other Provinces; it certainly is the best and most effective seed and demonstration farm I have seen in India.

Modern agricultural implements are stocked by the farm and sold in fairly good numbers, the various Agricultural Associations acting as agents for the sale.

I strongly advise makers of agricultural implements to devote their attention to India; the opinion that the cultivators are very conservative and cannot be persuaded to adopt new methods, has to a great extent been proved a fallacy. From what I have seen of the Indian farmer, I think he is less conservative than his confrère in England. It is noteworthy to add that one large English firm of implement makers sent, last year, a practical man on an educational tour through India.

Soil and Methods of Cotton Cultivation.

The soil is a stiff loam known in India as "black cotton soil." It contains a high percentage of clay, and cracks freely in dry weather. Owing to these wide fissues, which one can notice all over the country in dry weather, it is a common saying in India that the black cotton soil ploughs itself. The cracking of the soil takes place immediately after the rains, *i.e.*, in November, and there-

Intercultivation in the south of Bombay Presidency.

fore quickly maturing kinds of cotton must be grown, as otherwise the roots of the plants get torn asunder owing to the cracking of the soil. For this purpose it is necessary to sow in June so that the bolls set towards the end of October. This accounts for the fact that the cotton soils in the Central Provinces are ploughed very seldom, I am told, only once in 10 years with the ordinary country plough. The usual method of preparing the soil is with the blade harrow (locally known as "bakhar"); this implement consists of a knife-like blade attached to a short wooden beam, which is drawn by a bullock, the cultivator pressing the blade into the soil. Thus it may be said that the surface soil is simply scraped. It is the custom to "bakhar" the fields in this manner two or three times during the hot weather, and then again just after the first rainfall, *i.e.*, immediately before sowing. The sowing is carried on in a very primitive manner. The sowing implement consists simply of three tubes or bamboo sticks fastened by string to a wooden beam and supported by the left hand whilst the seed is dropped into the tube by the right hand of the sower. The sowing is done on the flat in very straight lines, the drills being from 15in. to 20in. apart; the plants are generally thinned out to a distance of 6in. to 7in. It will be readily understood that in consequence of this primitive method of sowing a number of vacant spaces occur whenever the cultivator finishes the seed which he has in his hand. Sometimes the seed is held by a small cup attached to the top of the tube, and whenever this wants replenishing vacant spaces occur in the drill. Where the seed in a cotton field has not come up or where seed has not been put in through the fault of the sower, and when it is too late to replant cotton, it is the custom to dibble into the bare places "jowar" seed (millet).

Intercultivation (*i.e.*, loosening the soil between the rows) is carried on by a similar blade-harrow instrument closely resembling the "bakhar" already described. In this case two or three implements are worked by one pair of bullocks. Each field is intercultivated four or five times until the bolls begin to form.

Sowing begins about the third week in June and the picking begins somewhere about the third week in October. Buri, bani and other exotic kinds of cotton generally take 14 days longer to mature; the fields are picked over every three weeks, the first picking contains a higher percentage of bolls affected by boll worm. The second and third pickings in the Central Provinces give the best lint and seed; four or five pickings are generally obtainable, the last taking place in January. It is very strange that in many other Provinces of India the first picking is the best, whilst here the second and third are decidedly superior. As early as February the cultivator begins to prepare his land for the following year's crop.

The wages paid for picking cotton are 5 annas per 40lbs., and one woman can pick on an average 45lbs. per day. Until quite recently it was the general custom for the pickers to receive a certain quantity of the cotton picked, say one-twentieth, in lieu of wages.

On the Government Farms the wages for permanent labourers are 8 rupees per month during eight months of the year and 9 rupees per month during the four harvest months. In Berar labourers often hire themselves out for the whole year, in which case they receive 70 to 80 rupees in cash at the beginning of their employment and some small portions of green crops during the year.

No strict rotation of crops is adhered to; in some cases, on the rich lands near the villages, the cultivators will grow cotton year after year without rotating with any other crop. The following remarks on this subject by the Deputy Director of Agriculture are very interesting:—

"Rotation experiment with *jari* cotton as the principal crop. The plots are manured with cattle dung at the rate of 40lbs. of nitrogen per acre in the year in which cotton is grown except in the case of plot IX. In plots III. and IV. there are six lines of cotton to two lines of *tur*.

" Area of each plot ·10 of an acre.

No. of plot.	Crop in 1907-08.	Outturn per acre in 1907-08. Seed cotton or grain.	Outturn per acre in 1907-08. Fodder.	Crop in 1908-09.	Outturn per acre in 1908-09. Seed cotton or grain.	Outturn per acre in 1908-09. Fodder.	Crop in 1909-10.	Outturn per acre in 1909-10. Seed cotton or grain.	Outturn per acre in 1909-10. Fodder.	Crop in 1910-11.	Outturn per acre in 1910-11. Seed cotton or grain.	Outturn per acre in 1910-11. Fodder.	Average value of outturn for four years.
		lbs.	lbs.		lbs.	lbs.		lbs.	lbs.		lbs.	lbs.	Rs. a. p.
I.	Cotton ..	160	—	Wheat ..	410	670	Cotton ..	467	—	Wheat ..	520	750	34 13 9
II.	Wheat ..	35	285	Cotton ..	150	—	Wheat ..	304	376	Cotton ..	293	—	22 6 8
III. .. {	Cotton ..	137		—	—	—	Cotton ..	215	—	—	—	—	}
	—	—	—	*Juar*	220	1,300	—	—	—	*Juar*	465	1,300	22 11 3
	Tur	76	70	—	—	—	*Tur*	200	240	—	—	—	}
IV. .. {	—	—		Cotton ..	97	—	—	—	—	Cotton ..	132	—	}
	Juar	410	1,910	—	—	—	*Juar*	531	2,045	—	—	—	27 15 7
	—		—	*Tur*	62	72	—	—	—	*Tur*	330	260	}
V.	Cotton ..	160		Gram.. ..	340	580	Cotton ..	441	—	Gram.. ..	544	736	28 15 7
VI.	Gram.. ..	270	300	Cotton ..	267	—	Gram.. ..	315	515	Cotton ..	384	—	30 10 8
VII.. ..	Cotton ..	182		*Tur*	350	102	Cotton ..	558		*Tur*	515	415	30 7 6
VIII. ..	*Tur*	340	415	Cotton ..	279		*Tur*	345	389	Cotton ..	358		32 9 1
IX	Cotton ..	147		Cotton ..	277		Cotton ..	601	—	Cotton ..	348	—	40 0 7

Tur = Cazanius indicus. Gran = Cicer arietenum. Juar = Millet.

"In Berar cotton occupied 41 per cent. of the cropped area last year. There is a good deal of variation in the rotations practised. The commonest is cotton followed by *juar*, cotton being sown as a mixed crop with *tur* in the proportion of from 12 to 20 lines of cotton to two of *tur*. The *juar* of the rotation is grown entirely for local consumption.

"The cotton-wheat and cotton-gram rotations are practised to some extent in the deep black soil of the Purna valley, which is very retentive of moisture, and which therefore lends itself to the cultivation of *rabi* crops.

"Cotton followed by *tur* is very seldom practised except in the poorer parts of Morsi and the Melghat Taluks.

"Cotton cultivation continuously in the same field for a period of years, as in plot No. IX., has become a fairly common practice in Berar. This disregard of the principle of rotation in cropping is decried by scientists, who attribute to it the spread of insect pests and fungoid diseases. The results up to date, however, have not justified that assumption. The experiment has now gone on for four years; no trace of disease and no serious damage by insect pests have yet been noticed. Economically the practice has proved a sound one owing to the high price of cotton, and it is therefore being followed in the non-experimental area of the farm."

Many other highly interesting experiments are carried on by the Deputy Directors on the Government farms, the results of which are published yearly in the annual reports of the Agricultural Stations, and I would recommend the study of these to all Colonial cotton-growing companies. Copies of all the Government publications on agriculture may be bought at cheap rates at the following booksellers:—

Constable & Co., 10, Orange Street, Leicester Square, London, W.C.

P. S. King & Son, 9, Bridge Street, Westminster, London, S.W.

Friedlander & Sohn, 11, Carlstrasse, Berlin.

Ernest Leroux, 28, Rue Bonaparte, Paris.

Ginneries.

The *ginneries* are mostly in the hands of native firms. The cost of ginning at any of the ordinary ginneries is 3-4 rupees per 280lbs. lint; pressing costs rupees 2. 8. 0. per bale. I inspected five ginning factories in the Central Provinces; all were in a disorderly condition, the loose bales in the yard were often open at one end, and no care was taken to prevent the cotton becoming dirtied by the dust. I was specially struck with the great amount of loose cotton lying about in the yards of the ginneries. Everywhere is waste of labour; the cotton is carried from a huge stack to the gin by coolies, and when ginned it is swept out of the gin on to a platform where sacks are hung up and filled with cotton by men who press it down with their feet. Instead of automatic transporters for cotton seed which one sees at many gins in India, women carry it in buckets on their heads to the yard, a distance of about 100 yards from the factory.

Watering of Cotton for the Purpose of Fraudulently Increasing Its Weight.

The most interesting thing from a spinner's point of view which I saw at one of the ginneries in Akola was the artificial watering of cotton. My attention to the watering of the cotton in the Central Provinces and Berar had been directed by various cotton ginners and spinners in different districts throughout India, which is proof that the fraudulent methods are extensive and well known. I must confess that in no other Province have I found such glaring frauds carried on as in Akola; evidently no secret is made of the watering, because when I asked one of the ginners the reason why the whole of his yard was covered with water pipes, he acknowledged at once

WATERING GINNED COTTON AT AKOLA,
In order to increase the weight.

that they were there in the first instance for the purpose of protecting the cotton against fire, and in the second for the purpose of watering it. I was told that watering in the way depicted in the two accompanying illustrations is done at almost every ginning factory in Akola. No charge is made for this watering, and the owner of one gin told me that the cotton is watered only if the owner requests them to do so. There was no hesitation shown when I asked for a demonstration of the manner in which the cotton is watered. About six coolies got a hose-pipe ready—it was almost 3in. in diameter, and the nozzle had an opening of about 1in. diameter—several coolies mounted a heap of about 100 loose bales of ginned cotton, and the water was poured over them just as they would have done had the bales been on fire. The owner of the gin told me that it is customary to water in this manner for 20 minutes a lot of 100 bales. The cotton which had been watered on the previous night was absolutely "wringing wet," and although a certain amount of moisture will evaporate during exposure to the sun and during the process of final pressing, yet it must be evident that any spinner who receives such cotton is a heavy loser.

I have written a letter on this subject to Mr. C. E. Low, C.I.E., at Nagpur, who, besides being the Director of Agriculture, is also the Director of Industries, and I have pointed out to him that a great amount of the exceedingly fine work which he and his Agricultural Department perform, is bound to suffer through such fraudulent

WATERING GINNED COTTON AT AKOLA,
In order to increase the weight of the bales.

practices, and that this watering of cotton is just as much a criminal offence as the selling by wrong weights. I have also sent a photograph of this process of watering of cotton to the Member for Commerce and Industry, the Hon. W. H. Clarke, with whom I discussed the matter at Calcutta, and from correspondence I have received I can state that the question is being thoroughly investigated at present, and quite recently I have been informed that the Government has decided to stop this practice.

Some 40 years ago there was in existence in the Bombay Presidency a Cotton Fraud Act, which was, however, repealed, on the instigation of the Bombay and Manchester Chambers of Commerce. From what I can gather the cause of its repeal was the charge levied on every bale by the Government. From the evidence I was able to procure, I learnt that the Act had many beneficial results.

Whilst not advocating a levy per bale, I feel sure that the Government could prosecute in the case of watering such as described. It would be easy to prove the offence of watering the cotton, whilst in the case of mixing inferior with superior cottons the difficulty would be in proving the offence; but even there, owing to the number of people necessary for carrying out the mixing, the offence might be detected.

Manure.

Manures are more highly valued in the cotton tract than in any other part of the Province, nevertheless a large portion of the cattle dung, which is really the only manure used on a large scale, is made up in cakes and burnt as fuel. Unfortunately fuel is scarcer in the cotton tract than in other districts owing to the absence of forests. Manure as a rule is not used for cold weather crops (*rabi crops*) except in the case of irrigable garden lands. The Agricultural Department has been experimenting with "poudrette" (dry night soil), cattle urine, conserved by the dry earth system, and various nitrogenous fertilisers. The results of these experiments are given in the annual reports and are most instructive. Of all the manures tried "poudrette" has proved the most valuable; it is obtained only in the vicinity of large towns, where the municipality collects it in pits. There is, however, a great aversion against the use of this manure on the part of the natives, and none but the very lowest caste can be persuaded to use it. The nitrogenous fertilisers invariably give a considerable increase in the out-turn when applied to cotton grown on black soil, but the value of the increase is not commensurate with the cost of the manure. An application of cattle dung followed by a top dressing of nitrogenous fertilisers, such as nitrate of soda and saltpetre, has given distinctly promising results. The Agricultural Department is of the opinion that the cotton cultivator can best be assisted by showing him how to make a proper use of the locally obtainable manures, such as dung and urine of his cattle, and the dry earth system of conserving the latter is strongly recommended.

Causes of Mixing.

Besides the intentional mixing carried on in the ginning factories, there are a few causes which may not have been sufficiently considered. Cattle are largely fed on cotton seed; as much as 4-5lbs. per day are given, and some of the seed passes without being digested. Therefore it frequently happens that the dung contains whole seeds, and these, after being put on the fields with the dung, spring up and cause a mixture. It is also frequently the custom to send cattle into the fields after the last picking for the purpose of eating the cotton leaves. Another cause of mixture must be the late picking, *i.e.*, picking when the cotton is over-ripe, because the bolls begin to shed and some of the seed sows itself, and when another kind is sown in the next year two varieties are at once present.

Insect Pests.

The boll worm does not do as much damage in the Central Provinces as in the Punjab and other parts of India. It has been found that exotic cotton tried in isolated plots in non-cotton tracts are often severely damaged by boll worm and leaf caterpillars, but when these kinds are grown on larger areas the damage is much less severe. Bhindi (Hibiscus esculantus, or lady's finger) has been tried with success as a trap crop on the experimental farms, but it is doubtful whether it can be used with advantage by the cultivators in villages where there is little or no demand for "bhindi" as a vegetable. "Bhindi," or lady's finger, is preferred by the insects infesting the cotton plant, and as it comes into leaf before cotton, the insects collect in it; at that period the bhindi must be taken from the field and destroyed. Unless this vegetable is destroyed as soon as the insects appear, it will act as a breeding area for them. Bhindi seed is mixed with the cotton seed in the proportion of 1lb. bhindi to 100lbs. cotton seed.

Experiments are also being made with the parasite "Rogus Lefroyi," which destroys the boll worm by making its living place

The Cotton Market at Akola.

in the worm. In some Provinces these parasites have been to a certain extent successfully reared, but in others new parasites have attacked the boll worm parasite.

Buying Agencies.

In view of the intimate relationship existing between the Department of Agriculture of the Central Provinces and the cotton mills, especially with Messrs. Tatas' Empress Mills, whose public-spirited and able manager is Sir Bezonje Dadhaboi Metha, there is no need to establish a Buying Agency in the Province; all the more as the long staple cotton which is grown at present is only 1,500 bales. When the extension of Buri or Cambodia cotton in the Native States of Chhattisgarh has become an established fact it would no doubt be useful to make arrangements for the purchase of cotton on a guaranteed basis, but this will take a few years yet.

Cotton Markets.

It is customary for the farmers to bring their unginned cotton for sale to a cotton market. I visited the Akola Cotton Market, of which the accompanying photograph gives a good illustration; it was established some 10 or 12 years ago. It is open from 7 to 11 in the morning, and from the early hours the cultivators bring the seed cotton, mostly loose, in primitive carts to this market. For each cart a levy of 1d. is charged by the Municipal Committee. Five members of the Town Council are appointed to act as a committee on the cotton market. Each cultivator has his own agent, who shows the samples to buyers. When a price has been agreed upon the cotton is delivered and weighed on a beam balance. The agent (adhatia) generally pays cash in the evening of the transaction to the cultivator, whilst he himself receives the money from the buyer on the following day. The commission to the "adhatia" is 1 rupee per cart. The price of the cotton is fixed almost solely on the ginning out-turn and the colour; the length of staple is generally left out of consideration. In the busy season as many as 5,200 carts of cotton change hands in one day in the Akola Market.

BOMBAY PRESIDENCY.

There are five Cotton Tracts in this Presidency, viz. :—

	Soil	Rainfall
		inches
1. The Surtee-Broach or South Gujarat Tract	Black clay	33-45
2. The Ahmedabad-Kaira or North Gujarat Tract	Sandy	28-37
3. The Karnatak Tract...	Black clay	23-34
4. The Deccan Tract	...	20-30
5. The Sind Tract	Loam	7.0

with a yearly total area under cotton of nearly eight million acres.

I.—SURTEE-BROACH DISTRICT.

The principal towns in this district are Surat, Nausari, Broach. The general aspect of the country is that of a flat plain relieved by a scattered growth of bàbul (Acacia arabica), toddy palm (Phœnix sylvestris), and other trees.

The soil is deep black and retentive, which under a rainfall of 34in. to 45in., within a period of 3½ months, can support the best indigenous cotton, which requires eight months to mature.

The cotton of this district is that well known as Surtee-Broach. It is noteworthy that the quality of the cotton produced, known commercially as "Broach," improves as we proceed south, Nausari, near the southern boundary of the tract, producing the finest staple of the growth.

The crop is sown in a two-year rotation with Jowar (Sorghum), with the first rains in the middle of June; picking takes place in February-March. The cultivators are probably the most careful in India.

In parts of certain talukas (village districts) in the north of the tract (viz., Jambusar and A'mod) a coarser variety of the herbaceum species known as "Goghari" is also sown partly on light soil. This is doubtless fraudulently mixed with the finer growth. The growing of an inferior style of cotton in an area suited to and bordering on a finer growth is a matter of considerable importance when the improvement of the staple of the tract as a whole is taken up. The Indian ginner seems to be unable to resist the temptation of mixing a low quality with a superior one.

The cotton grown generally in this district is Surat "Deshi" Broach of ⅝in. staple; the yield on one acre of the Government Farm of plants raised from ordinary Bazaar seed was 498lbs. of seed cotton, with a ginning out-turn of 32·9 per cent.

Method of Cultivation.

Instead of a plough a scraper, as described in the previous pages, is used to loosen the soil prior to the arrival of the monsoon. Ploughing with steel ploughs is only recommended when it is a question of getting rid of the deep-rooted weeds, and then it must be done at once after the rains, the ground being heavy black soil, which it would be impossible to plough in dry weather.

Many parts of India are suffering from a deep-rooted weed called "heriali" (Cynodon dactylon). In the south of the Bombay Presidency I was very pleased to see that a plough had been obtained by the Government with the special view of assisting farmers to get rid of this deep-rooted weed, which soon spreads over the whole field. The plough in question was made by A. Bajac, Liancourt, France, and was worked by means of two windlasses; it is designed on the system of the steam plough, a windlass is fixed on either side of the field, a cable to which is fastened the plough is wound up by one windlass and let out by the other. The windlass is turned either by two strong bullocks or four medium-sized ones. The illustration given here shows the implement. The total cost is 3,200 rupees, delivered in India, and the whole of the machinery appeared exceedingly well made. The plough moves slowly from one end of the field to the other, but does the work efficiently. One-quarter of an acre is ploughed in 8 hours. I have measured the depth of a furrow, and found it to be almost 16in. The Agricultural Department hires this plough out to farmers at a charge of 3 rupees per day, and it is a sign of the advancement amongst the cultivators that they have readily taken up this implement. I was told that this plough is booked already for every day during the next three years. Cultivators have been driven to the necessity of digging up their fields owing to the rapid spreading of the weed. The cost of the labour for digging up the field is calculated at 50 rupees per acre. With a Bajac plough, if they hire the bullocks, the clearing costs them 28 rupees per acre, the farmer finding the labour. The plough can be easily worked.

I consider that the Agricultural Departments or the Co-operative Credit Societies and the local Boards should supply these ploughs in the various Provinces, as it cannot be expected that the farmer will invest so much money as is required. This is certainly a practical kind of work, and would cause a very large area of land in India to be made cultivable.

Plough supplied by A. BAJAC, LIANCOURT (FRANCE). The plough works 15 to 16 inches deep and is driven by bullocks by means of a windlass on either side of the field, on the system of a steam plough.

Sowing. After the first break of the monsoon, when about 4-5in. of rain has fallen, the field is sown on the flat in perfectly straight lines, 2ft. apart. A sowing drill similar to that already described is employed. The plants are thinned out to about 12in. apart as soon as they are about 6in. high. The soil is loosened by the intercultivator, the scraping implement as described previously. It is quite remarkable how straight the lines are sown; the hoeing by means of the intercultivator prevents the cracking of the heavy soil and thus the evaporation of moisture.

Sowing takes place in July and extends to September if necessary; 10lbs. of seed are required per acre. There is hardly any irrigated cotton in the Bombay Presidency. A great number of draw-wells exist; the cost of the one illustrated is 1,500 rupees.

Manure. The supply of stable manure is very limited because only one pair of cattle is kept for every 20 or 30 acres. A good cultivator will keep a buffalo for milk and manure, but will never work the cow. During about five months (*i.e.*, principally the dry season) the cow manure is made into cakes and used as fuel. This is a very serious question of agriculture. No artificial manure can be used at the present prices. There is hardly any litter used in the stables, and therefore the manure is very rich.

A WELL NEAR SURAT.

(Whilst the bullocks walk down the incline the bucket ascends; no water is lifted whilst the bullocks walk up the hill.)

Rotations of Crop. Generally, a two-years' rotation of crops is practiced in this district, viz., *sorghum,* with a mixture of *tur* (pigeon-pea, Cazanius indicus), which is a leguminous crop, and the following year cotton. Sorghum is used as a grain food for the people, and the stems serve as fodder for the cattle. Lately it has been found that ground-nuts are an excellent rotation crop, but there are some difficulties as regards harvesting. The jackals, which abound in India, do a great deal of harm to the ground-nuts.

Insect Pests. Generally speaking, the cotton of this district is comparatively free from insects. There certainly are boll-worm, asphis, and a surface caterpillar, but none of them is serious except during the cloudy weather at the back-end of the season.

Picking.

Women are engaged in the picking; they are able to gather about 40lbs. a day, for which they receive 3d. If the work is carried out by contract as much as 100lbs. can be collected, but dirt, leaves, and other impurities are mixed up with the cotton picked. Scarcity of labour is seriously felt during the picking season, although Gujarat has a population of 419 per square mile, and is one of the most thickly-populated agricultural districts in India.

Mode of Selling Crop

It is customary for dallals (small merchants) to personally visit the villages for the purpose of collecting the cotton. Cultivators who are in need of money receive advances from them. Any verbal agreement, unless supported by token, is not regarded as binding.

Ginneries.

There are more ginning factories in the district than are really wanted, and the various firms have now amalgamated, closed some of the old gins, and the profits of all are pooled and then divided. Only a few of the gins at Surat possess steam presses; in many cases the loose bales of ginned cotton have to be sent by rail to the steam press. I was told that it does not pay to have a steam press in connection with a ginning factory unless 5,000 bales are turned out per season. The charge for ginning is rupees 4. 8. 0. per bhar of 916lbs.; the seed belongs to the cultivator. There is practically no hand ginning done in the Bombay Presidency.

Bombay Millowners' Buying Agency.

The Bombay Millowners have established a buying agency in Surat to stimulate the growing of an improved Broach cotton. They have not considered it advisable to erect their own ginnery, but have found it more advantageous to hire one of the existing gins. The accompanying photograph of this ginnery was taken some time before the season started, and shows the place perhaps to a disadvantage. All the gins in this ginnery are somewhat old but still in working condition. The ginneries in this district work generally from February to the beginning of April, and one factory with 30 gins last season turned out about 4,000 bhars of 916lbs. of seed cotton equal to about 3,000 bales lint. The owner of the ginning factory which attends to the cotton of the Bombay Millowners' Buying Agency has given an undertaking that the seed will be kept perfectly separate. The drawback with the working of this gin seems to me to be the long distance which in some cases separate it from the cotton fields where this special cotton is grown. The half-pressed bales of this ginning factory have to be sent by train to Broach in order to be steam-pressed there. This means an additional expense of 2 rupees per bale, viz., 1 rupee for carriage and 1 rupee for pressing. During this season 2,300 bales of the improved

Broach cotton will be produced, and it is anticipated that next season, if the farmers are satisfied with the price obtained, 20,000 bales will be grown. In this case an up-to-date ginnery will be hired for about eight weeks. The Bombay Millowners have guaranteed the farmers 5 per cent. above the price of the ordinary local cotton for the improved Broach, and, unfortunately for the spinners, as the difference in price between American and East Indian cotton has this season been very slight, they are likely to lose on the transaction.

The ginning factories are to a large extent in the hands of financially substantial people, and many of the Bombay traders are interested in them.

THE GINNERY AT SURAT
At which the Cotton for the Bombay Millowners' Buying Agency is Ginned.

Land Tenure

Practically speaking, there are only small landowners in Gujarat who hold 20 acres and possess on an average two pairs of cattle. The yearly assessment for the best cotton soil is about 7 rupees. This system is more or less that of a leasehold with an annual chief-rent of 7 rupees. The farmers may sublet the land, in which case rents as high as 17 rupees are obtained. Most of the cultivators have borrowed money at a high rate of interest (16 to 20 per cent.), but the loans received are not very large. I was told that about 15 per cent. of the farmers who grew the improved Broach cotton required advances from the Bombay Millowners before the crops were matured.

There is no agricultural bank in the district, but Co-operative Credit Societies have been started. Since 1903 their number in the whole Bombay Province has increased to 350, and they are likely to make steady progress. The Co-operative Credit Societies have no central fund, but a central land bank has been established recently in Bombay for the purpose of financing Co-operative Credit Societies in the sugar cane tract. This central land bank is a private concern, guaranteed by the Government. It lends to Co-operative Societies at 7 per cent. per annum, and the farmer receives the loan from the latter at 9 per cent. per annum.

Wages.

The wages have already risen, and, owing to the scarcity of labour which is making itself felt, there is likely to be a further advance. At present the wages are: Men 4d., women 3d., children 2d. per day of eight hours.

Extension of cotton area. Increase of yield and improvement of quality.

There is no further area in this district—in fact, hardly any in the whole of the Bombay Presidency—which might be put under cotton. It seems, therefore, that as regards the area the Bombay Presidency has reached its limit, but the yield could be materially increased by:—

(1) Clearing the land thoroughly of the deep-rooted weeds, as described previously.

(2) By seed selection, inferior types must be removed by separating the best strains and selecting within the latter. There is a much larger staff required for seed distribution. I am convinced that if the seed farm system of the Central Provinces were introduced into Gujarat some considerable progress would be achieved, as the people of the district are very intelligent.

(3) Better rotation of crops, if necessary three years' rotation, say, cotton, sorghum, and sesamen (oil seed).

(4) Manuring more judiciously.

In the native State of Kathiawar 12 years ago a nice cotton, known by the trade name of "Dhollera," was grown. This has now been replaced by a very inferior cotton called "Mathio," which is a high yielder and early maturing.

Surat Government Farm.

I paid a visit to this farm, which has 315 acres, 165 of which are arable, the remainder being pasture. The farm is well managed.

A great many improved strains of cotton have been raised, but special attention is now given to the following three:—

(1) Selected Surat.
(2) Hybrid 1018.
(3) Hybrid 1027.

These cottons have yielded well, and their ginning percentage is also satisfactory. On land in good condition selected Surat gave an out-turn of 692lbs. seed cotton, with a ginning percentage of 32·2 The Hybrid 1027 yielded at the rate of 575lbs., with a ginning outturn of 33·8 per cent., and Hybrid 1018 yielded 546lbs., with a ginning out-turn of 34·6 per cent. The following valuations of large samples by Lancashire spinners may be of interest :—

Name of variety	* Valuations of one Firm on 23rd September	† Valuations of another Firm on October 26th
Selected Surat ...	Fully good to fine Broach. Price 7d.	7¾d.
1018 P/G	Beautiful Staple, could easily be spun to 20s. twist, 26s. weft. Price 6½d.	7½d.
1027-A., L. & F.	Could be used for weft, would spin up to 22/24. If mixed with American cotton could be spun up to 30s. Price 6⅞d. for "spot."	7¼d.

* Middling American was quoted at 7·61d. per pound on 30th September in Liverpool.

† Middling American quotation on October 26th was 7·88 and that of fine Broach 7½d. in Liverpool.

Last year some 3,000 acres were sown with these cottons by cultivators in the neighbourhood of the Government Farm, and the Department organised a sale by auction of the seed cotton. The seed which has been produced on the Government Farm is now known in the Bazaar as "farm cotton," which is an important factor.

It is not astonishing that the farmers who have grown small quantities of these new hybrids have not yet been able to obtain a fair price for their produce. A buyer has no special use for, say, 20lbs. superior cotton when he is purchasing at the same time 400lbs. of ordinary cotton from the same farmer. The cost of collecting the many small lots of this higher-grade cotton must be very heavy, and I am inclined to think that the Department has made a mistake in persuading the cultivators to grow these new strains before sufficient seed was obtainable to produce a fair marketable quantity. It also seems to me that experiments are carried on with too many varieties, and I think it would be more judicious for the Agricultural Department to concentrate its attention on one or two kinds and hand the seed of these over to the cultivators, after their suitability has been established beyond doubt, and after a sufficient quantity of seed is available to produce, say, a few thousand bales of each. In this way a natural demand would spring up, and the supply would not require to be "nursed" by a guarantee from a buying agency.

II.—AHMEDABAD-KAIRA OR NORTH GUJARAT DISTRICT.

This tract, comprising the two districts indicated by its name, together with the northern part of the Broach district, is somewhat remarkable in that it grows within a narrow area a number of types in a more or less mixed condition. This is due partly to the black soil occurring in patches and partly to the use of well irrigation. The average rainfall is 30in. The four chief types of cotton grown are known to cultivators as *Wagad, Lalia, Goghari,* and *Rozi.* Commercially they are grouped under the common name of "*Dhollera.*" The growth is largely consumed locally in the mills of Ahmedabad.

Wagad is a variety of *herbaceum* differing from the broach outwardly only in size. The peculiarity with regard to this cotton is that the bolls are bodily plucked from the plants, and the seed cotton is extracted at leisure in the houses of the cultivators. The cotton is of a fair quality, coarser than Lalia, but owing to the primitive method of harvesting, Wagad contains more dirt and other impurities.

Lalia is identical with Broach, and under well-irrigation yields a similar cotton. This kind and the previous one are frequently mixed together.

Goghari is grown unirrigated under the same conditions as unirrigated Lalia. It produces a coarser fibre, but yields better on a short rainfall.

Rozi is a *perennial,* and once sown is left on the land for three or four years. Generally, there is a mixed crop (Cereals) on the same field. The ginning out-turn is only 25 per cent., and the quality of the cotton is also inferior.

The yield per acre in this district varies from 200lbs. seed cotton when unirrigated to as much as 1,200lbs. when irrigated.

The Government farm in this district is situated at Nadiad, but not much attention is given to cotton. Experiments with perennial cotton are still continued there. These require water in the first year to get established; in the second year the trees have given 1,000lbs. seed cotton per acre, yielding about 300lbs. lint, but the third year the yield goes down to 600lbs. The Deputy Director estimates that 2,000 bales of cotton of the perennial kind might be produced in this district. The staple is long, but, as far as I remember, it is very irregular. As I have pointed out in my first report, I cannot see the advisability of growing these perennial cottons, because they harbour insect pests in the bark, and the branches are so brittle that they get easily damaged by the wind. Many experts have again given me their opinion that tree cotton should everywhere in India be given up.

III.—THE DECCAN TRACT.

The soil is a black clay, and the rainfall about 40in. in the East and 20 inches in the West. It is adjoining Berar in the East. The northern part is called Kandesh; it produces a *Neglectum* mixture consisting of five varieties. In the East one million acres are under cotton, in the West about 500,000. All cotton grown here is of an inferior kind, and the Government has endeavoured to separate the different varieties, and to select those with the highest ginning out-turn.

400lbs. seed cotton is a good average yield.

Assessment is rupees 1. 8. 0. to 2 rupees per acre; when land is rented 12 rupees are paid.

Most of the tenants own from 5-25 acres, but there are some farms as large as 100 acres.

The prepondering variety of cotton is *Rosea,* with a staple of $\frac{3}{8}$in. to $\frac{1}{2}$in. Its colour is very bright and white.

South of this district is Deccan proper. Although cotton here is planted on a somewhat extensive scale, it cannot be considered a lucrative crop. I did not visit this district, but was told that the Government is giving more attention to the cultivation of sugar cane than of cotton. Some increased area should be put under cotton as soon as the irrigation canals, under construction at present, are finished, and it is hoped that the Agricultural Department will then devote more attention to cotton.

IV.—THE KARNATAK TRACT.

Kinds of Cotton.

The important places in this tract are Dharwar, Gadag, Hubli. The soil in the western district is red, and rice is the staple crop; very little cotton is grown there. The black soil tract is east of the railway, known as black cotton soil under the name of "Desh." Here the staple crops are cotton, jowar, and wheat; 5/600,000 acres are under cotton, of which about 200,000 acres produced Dharwar-American cotton. This has a $\frac{5}{8}$in. to $\frac{3}{4}$in. staple, a nice colour, and a ginning out-turn of 30 per cent.; its yield is 200lbs. seed cotton in the East and 300lbs. in the West. The other kind of cotton grown is *Kumpta;* its staple is $\frac{3}{4}$in. to $\frac{7}{8}$in.; it has a dull fibre, but the quality is possibly somewhat finer than Broach, of which it is an offspring. Unfortunately, the ginning out-turn is only 27 per cent.; it yields 300-400lbs. per acre. It is estimated that 29,000 bales of Dharwar-American and 60,000 bales of Kumpta will be picked early this year. It is interesting to note that, whilst these yields are very low, the Government farms at Dharwar and Gadag have produced as much as 900lbs. seed cotton. The Agricultural Department is pushing Broach in the most favoured parts of the Kumpta tract, because it has a higher ginning percentage, viz., 33 per cent., and is better in colour. Broach must be sown in the Karnatak district with the early rains. The staple of the cotton shown to me was $\frac{7}{8}$in., and the fibre was a pure white. Dharwar-American had only a $\frac{5}{8}$in. staple, and is not very strong. The Department is replacing it by Cambodia in the dry districts. Broach and Cambodia can naturally be picked cleaner, as the bolls are more open and are larger than those of Dharwar cotton. The Government Department has raised the ginning out-turn of Broach in this district to 34 per cent., and at the auction sale the Broach cotton of this district was sold at 220 rupees per *naga* of 1,344lbs. seed cotton, whilst Kumpta on the same day was bought at 150/154 rupees per naga. During the last three years auction sales were held by the Agricultural Department for the disposal of this improved cotton in order to secure fair value. The whole of the produce was sold last year to two Indian Millowners, and on an average fetched 12 per cent. above the price of Kumpta. 1,000 acres were under Broach cotton in the Karnatak Tract during 1910/11 season, and produced 170 *nagas*.

There is no organisation for seed distribution in existence on anything like the lines of those successfully adopted in the Central Provinces. The Broach seed used for distribution is obtained in the Gujarat district (north of Bombay Presidency) from selected fields. There is no seed farm for pure Kumpta cotton, except a small area on the Dharwar farm.

I have no faith in rearing seed from selected fields belonging to the farmers. When the Deputy Director of Agriculture and I visited a Cambodia field near Hubli, it was demonstrated to us that the system of buying seed from the farmer, although the field may be considered pure, is a mistaken one. We saw in a field for which the seed had been supplied by the Agricultural Department that Dharwar-American and Kumpta cotton were growing mixed with the Cambodia cotton. Within an area of 20 square yards we could clearly distinguish about 12 plants of Dharwar or Kumpta cotton amongst the Cambodia. Seed farms must be under constant Government inspection. I have tried to persuade the Deputy Director as well as the Director to establish a few "*nucleus*" seed farms and a number of small seed farms in the whole of the Bombay Presidency. It must always be remembered that these are no expense to the Government, and that they ensure, not only a supply of pure seed, but act at the same time as demonstration farms.

Land is held on the Ryotwari system. More than half the land is owned in areas of 5-25 acres. Some owners sublet it at a higher price than the assessment, which is only rupees 2. 8. 0. to 3. 0. 0. It is anticipated that the new assessment which will shortly come into force will be about 33 per cent. higher.

One farmer told me that he holds 13 acres of land which he has on a 10 years' lease for an annual payment of 51 rupees, the landowner paying the assessment on the condition that the tenant would clear the land of the deep-rooted weed. If the land had been cleared of the weed the cultivator would have had to pay 250 rupees for the 13 acres. The tax on the land in question was 3 rupees per acre.

The farmers are not so intelligent and careful as those in Gujarat, but in the Karnatak Tract they are better than those in the Deccan. Only a few Agricultural Associations are in existence, but the Co-operative Credit Societies seem to make progress.

Preparation. Cotton is usually preceded by jowar (Millet). The stubble of the jowar is broken up by a harrow in hot weather. A good cultivator will give the land a light ploughing about 4in. deep with the country plough. This takes place about the middle of June, *i.e.*, at the beginning of the monsoon. Cotton receives only the residue of manure from the preceding jowar crop. After ploughing, one or two harrowings with the *bakha* are given. Cotton is sown in August with the primitive sowing drill already described. Many blanks are left in the drills; 7-8lbs. of cotton seed are used for one acre, and it is customary in this district to mix with the seed castor cold weather-jowar, line seed, &c., in very small quantities. No thinning-out takes place; the drills are 18in. apart, and the soil is loosened by the intercultivator. The weeds are removed from between the plants after the first intercultivation. In case of a slight rain at the beginning of November, a light ploughing is applied instead of the last intercultivation. The flowers begin to show about the middle of January, and then the field is left entirely alone until the picking season, which begins in March and lasts until the middle of April. There are about four pickings, the first and second being the best. Picking wages are paid in kind. The pickers receive one-eighth to one-twelfth for the first three pickings, and one-fourth of the last picking. The picking is carried out most carelessly, and often the cotton is allowed to shed. It is a great mistake to pay the pickers in kind, because the cotton which the pickers receive, is afterwards taken to the petty merchant in the village, who mixes all the different kinds together in his store. I was told that it is the general practice for the small grower in this district

PLOUGHING IN INDIA.

(Notice the stone on the plough to increase the pressure.)

to moisten the canvas in which he packs his cotton, and that frequently water is poured over the bale before it is sent to the market. My informant also told me that water is added after ginning, especially in the Barsi district.

There is no extension of area likely in the Dharwar district, but the yield can be materially improved by good cultivation and selected seed.

Insects have not caused great damage, although in the Dharwar district the boll-worm makes itself occasionally felt.

Hubli has a cotton market similar to Akola in the Central Provinces. The brokers (" Dallals ") sell the cotton for the cultivator, charging him 1 rupee 4 annas per naga of 1,344lbs., and the buyer 12 annas. When the broker makes an advance to the cultivator he charges from 9 to 15 per cent. interest.

I may mention that the Japanese Millowners have a buying agency in this district.

Ginneries.

The ginneries are in the hands of local people. The charge is 5 to 7 rupees per 336lbs. lint for ginning, including loose baling and canvas. I was assured that watering at the gin is done in Barsi, just the same as in Akola, Central Provinces. The steam presses for export bales at Hubli, Gadag, and Dharwar charge 3 rupees to 4 rupees per bale, of about 382lbs. to 400lbs. The price of seed at the time of my enquiry was 40lbs. for 1 rupee. The ginners in this district do not as a rule buy cotton; there are a few merchants who also own ginning factories where they gin their own cotton. There is an abundance of gins, and in case a buying agency were to be established at some time in this district there would be no difficulty in hiring a gin for the whole season.

Mixing of Cotton.

It is a common practice for the cultivators to mix Broach with Kumpta cotton, and the ginners mix Dharwar-American and Kumpta in order to get a good colour and consequently more profit. It is also the custom to bring inferior cotton from the Deccan district to be ginned at Hubli and Gadag, where it is mixed with Kumpta. I have been assured on good authority that even waste (fly) for mixing purposes is brought by merchants from the Bombay and Ahmedabad mills to the Hubli ginning factories. For the purpose of better mixing the waste is passed through an opener, together with seed-cotton.

Profit on Cotton Growing.

In conversation with an educated cultivator I gathered that he made 15 rupees per acre profit on his cotton. He estimated the cost of cultivation, seed, bullocks at 13 rupees, rent 12 rupees = 25 rupees per acre, the average crop being 400lbs. seed-cotton, which at the present price is sold for 40 rupees, therefore a profit of 15 rupees per acre.

Visit to Small Ginnery at Dharwar.

The following details which I obtained from the owner of a small gin depicted in the accompanying photograph may be of interest :—

A 16 h.p. oil engine works four double roller gins. The oil engine uses 3lbs. of oil every three hours, and works 12 hours per day during 3½ to 4 months in the year. The capacity of each double gin is about 800lbs. lint per day. The repairs on the whole plant come to 240 rupees per season. He charges for 336lbs. lint (resulting from a "naga" of 1,344lbs. seed-cotton) 5 rupees, including loose baling, packing, and weighing. The loose bales weigh 166lbs. The net profit during the last season, when 500 "nagas" were ginned altogether, came to 1,500 rupees. The total cost of the primitive ginning factory was 6,500 rupees, and an annual rent for the land of 60 rupees is charged. The owner works the oil engine, employs 16 to 18 women, who receive 4d. per day, and two men, with a wage of 6d. per day. Cotton is only ginned on commission. The owner does not buy or speculate in cotton.

Dharwar Government Farm.

On the *Dharwar Government farm,* which is well managed, the following Indian cottons are grown experimentally. They are fairly representative of the whole of India :—

Rozi (G. obtusiflorum).—A perennial cotton, grown in rows of 5ft. apart, with cereal crop in between. The plant is pruned back to

SMALL GINNERY AT DHARWAR.

Cost of Oil Engine (16-H.P.), Four Gins and Building, about £433 = Rs. 6,500. 800 lbs. of Lint Cotton are ginned daily in the season.

the soil every year. It has a harsh inferior fibre, and is grown in the north of Gujarat on light soil. Only very small quantities are produced ⅝in. staple. White.

Nadam.—Botanically same as Rozi; grown in Madras on light soil.

Deo Kapas (G. arboreum).—This is a tree that is usually grown near temples. The cotton from it is used for spinning sacred thread.

Kumpta.—G. herbaceum, grown in Dharwar.

Broach.—G. herbaceum, grown in Broach, and latterly in Dharwar.

Ghogari.—Noted for high ginning out-turn, is of a bright white colour, but its staple is shorter than that of Broach, grown in north of Broach district.

Wagad (G. herbaceum).—An annual grown in Ahmedabad and parts of Kathiawar; it is hardy and stands the frost. Bolls are collected in the field and taken to the houses, where the cotton is picked.

Bani (G. indicum).—Grown in Hinganghat, Central Province; an annual; fine beautiful fibre, full inch, but possessing only 27 per cent. ginning out-turn and a small yield per acre. It has a special soapy feel.

Jari (G. neglectum).—Grown in Central Province, Kandesh, Deccan, United Provinces. This neglectum variety is the most widely distributed cotton over India.

Mathio (G. neglectum).—Grown in Kathiawar, and has been substituted for that formerly well-known Dhollerah cotton. It is very poor, but has a high ginning out-turn and matures early.

Warhadi (G. neglectum roseum) has a high ginning out-turn and yield per acre, is early maturing, $\frac{3}{8}$in. fibre, coarse, very bright, liked for export, grown in Central Province, and Kandesh.

Comilla (G. cernuum).—Grown in Assam on Kil Hill, Garrow Hill. Very large ginning out-turn, 50 to 51 per cent., poor staple and coarse.

Kumpta (G. herbaceum).—South Maratha; good fibre and good staple, $\frac{3}{4}$in. to $\frac{7}{8}$in., strong, but dull. Low ginning out-turn, 27 to 29 per cent., fair yielder. This cotton is being replaced by the Agricultural Department with Broach. A great deal of dirt is always in the picked cotton.

On the Dharwar farm a 6½ h.p. Blackstone oil engine is kept. It is portable, and can be moved by one bullock. Its price was 1,600 rupees loco-Dharwar. The oil engine is principally used for driving a pump that lifts water from a depth of 30ft. During the ginning season this engine works a few small roller-gins on the farm, which turn out 34lbs. lint in one hour. The oil consumption of the engine is 1¾lbs. per hour.

The Dharwar farm has 130 acres, 70 of which are under cotton. It is an experimental farm for selection and hybridising and making manurial, tillage, and rotation experiments. I was told that the Government does not aim to make it self-supporting, which is, I think, an error, and if proper seed farms were added, I am convinced the whole undertaking might be made self-supporting, as is the case in the Central Provinces.

The best *manuring experiments* on the Dharwar farm were obtained with "*poudrette*," but here again the difficulties in its adoption, owing to caste, arise. I was told that the cultivators of sugar cane in the Poona district had sunk their aversion against "*poudrette*," but no doubt many years will elapse before the cultivators in the Dharwar district will follow their example.

It has been decided quite recently to nominate one of the native travelling teachers as extra Deputy Director of Agriculture, who is to have charge of the farms South of Poona. Mr. Main, the European Deputy Director, will confine his attention to the North of the Presidency, especially to Surat. I have no doubt that this appointment will be satisfactory. The principal part of the pioneer work has already been done unless it is decided that a seed farm is to be established.

Saw-gins versus Roller-gins.

At Hubli I inspected a few ginning factories which had both saw- and roller-gins. American cotton adheres firmer to the seed, and therefore saw ginning is considered necessary by the ginners of this district. Roller-gins remove linters as well from the seed, and it is necessary to run the rollers more slowly when ginning American cotton than when ginning Indian cotton. The saw-gins which I inspected were made by the Eagle Gin Company, Bridgewater, Mass. The shaft had 24 saws only, a fan blew the ginned cotton into an adjoining room, where it was collected and packed into loose bales. I had one and the same kind of cotton ginned by a roller-gin and a saw-gin. Certainly the saw-gin process turned out a much cleaner cotton. Hardly any impurities were left in it, whilst the roller-gin did not remove many of the impurities, such as parts of capsules, leaves, &c., but the staple of the cotton ginned by the roller-gin seemed to me considerably stronger. The Eagle saw-gin turns out about 30 per cent. more cotton than a roller-gin. I was told that *all* the Dharwar-American cotton is ginned by saw-gins, and that formerly Macarthy roller-gins had been in use, but owing to their low ginning capacity they had been entirely superseded by the Eagle gins. The cost of an Eagle saw-gin, with 24 saws on a shaft, placed at Hubli, is 350 rupees. Each gin requires 1 h.p. The cost of the double roller-gin placed at Hubli is 450 rupees. The price of ginning is 8d. per 28lbs. of lint (28lbs. are here called a maund), for Kumpta cotton on the double roller-gin, and 5¼d. per 28lbs. lint for Dharwar-American on a saw-gin.

The wages are 4½d. per 10 hours for women at the gin and 6d. per 10 hours for men for heavier work. At the height of the season 6d. and 9d. respectively are paid.

A native gentleman who showed me round various ginning factories told me that he could well remember Dharwar cotton being picked quite clean some 20 to 30 years ago, but owing to the fact that the wages are now paid on the quantity picked, the natives have become careless, and aim solely at a large weight.

One roller in a gin will last one season (about 100 days). When the grooves are made by hand they need not again be touched for four days, but when they are made by machinery they must be renewed once per day.

The bale presses are quite modern and up to date. Steam pressing at Hubli is charged at 4 rupees per bale. Usually the bale is pressed twice, first into what is called half-bales and then by the finishing press into export bales. I saw no watering done before pressing. The press turned out about 150 bales per day, the charge of 4 rupees per bale is inclusive of pressing, canvas, and hoops.

In order to remove more dust and impurities from ginned cotton, it is customary in this district to shake and beat it on a frame which is covered by a lattice work made of iron hoops. I have never seen cotton that was so freely mixed in the picking with dirt and impurities as in this locality. In one of the presses I saw a number of women mixing two different qualities of cotton by throwing the cotton into the air. It is here where waste cotton from the spinning mills is mixed with the seed-cotton for the purpose of deceiving the spinners abroad.

Gadag has also a cotton market. It differs from that of Akola in that each broker has his own store. All the stores are situated in one long street; in nearly every one there was some considerable quantity of cotton from last year's crop.

Most of the cultivators bring their seed-cotton in carts, but a few have their cotton ginned before marketing. In Gadag the cultivator sells through his broker to the petty merchant; the latter gins the seed-cotton and sells the fibre to the export merchant. The broker receives 8d. per 1,344lbs. unginned cotton, or per 336lbs. ginned cotton, from both the cultivator and the purchaser.

This district suffered severely last year from lack of rain. Only 12in. fell during June and July; there was no rain from then until October 10th, when another inch fell. Immediately after this last rainfall the cultivators put their cotton-seed into the ground, expecting the usual successive rains which unfortunately did not come. Consequently most of the fields looked in a deplorable condition, not only as regards cotton, but also as regards food crops.

Cotton is usually picked towards the end of February. Owing to this drought it is anticipated that the crop will only this year be 17 per cent. of the usual quantity.

Gadag Government Farm.

A very interesting demonstration in favour of ploughing for districts where the rain is uncertain was shown at the Gadag Government Farm. There was side by side a field prepared by the usual native scraper, and another ploughed with a steel plough to about 5 inches deep. Both fields were planted with Cambodia cotton, and the difference in crop in favour of the ploughed field was most marked. The superintendent of the farm thought it would yield 60 per cent. more than the field which had only been scraped. The preparation of the good field was one ploughing in May before the rains and 13 harrowings and one rolling afterwards; the inter-cultivator was used five times. The other field had been scraped five times in October, and received three intercultivations. Cambodia is making good headway all along this district, and the farmers confirm that Cambodia is a much better paying crop than Dharwar-American, which has been established here for many years. The yield of Cambodia is, however, small in comparison with that in Madras, viz., only 400lbs. seed-cotton per acre, but Dharwar-American yields only 200lbs. seed-cotton. The ginning out-turns for the two kinds were 38 per cent. Cambodia, and 29 per cent. Dharwar-American. The price of Cambodia cotton in this district last year was 205 rupees per 1,344lbs. seed-cotton, whilst that of Dharwar-American was only 175 rupees for the same weight. In spite of the drought, Cambodia has done better than the Dharwar-American cotton.

Hulkati. Some six miles from Gadag is situated a village called *Hulkati.* The cultivators of this village are growing nothing but Cambodia cotton, and they have recently bought an oil engine, and now gin their cotton themselves in order to keep their seed pure. These cultivators are extremely careful and intelligent. They recognise the advisability of proper treatment of the seed, and as there seems to exist the spirit of co-operation, proved by the purchase of the oil engine and gins, they should, in my opinion, receive some assistance from the Government. These people would undoubtedly respond quickly to any suggestion of improvements.

5,000lbs. Cambodia seed were sold last year, and 500 acres were sown with it. The seed was from plants raised in the district, and should be acclimatised.

Buying Agency. The Deputy Director is anxious that a buying agency for Cambodia cotton should be established in the district of Gadag. I told him that the first step towards such a buying agency would be for the Government to establish seed farms, and that, in view of the great demand for Cambodia cotton existing in the Madras Presidency, there should be no necessity for artificially stimulating the growth of Cambodia in Gadag, which is situated almost on the borders of the Madras Presidency.

V.—SIND.

The Province of Sind is in appearance very like Egypt, and its fertile soil has been created in a somewhat similar manner to that of the Egyptian Delta. The Indus River has been depositing silt during many thousands of years in this part of India, principally by inundations and by frequent changes of its course; even during the last few years this great river has altered its bed considerably. Sind is almost rainless, and the cultivator is therefore entirely dependent upon irrigation canals. Unfortunately the Sind canal system has not been constructed with a view to the extension of the agricultural area that has already taken place, and could still be continued. Briefly, the canals of Sind may be divided into two classes, viz., inundating and perennial. On canals of the latter kind, providing water all the year round, it has been proved that Egyptian and American cotton of qualities only slightly inferior to those of their countries of origin can be grown, and will yield as much seed-cotton as the local variety.

On the inundation canals, on the other hand, water is available only during the period of inundation of the Indus. This is about 3½ months (June to October), that is about the same as the period during which rain falls in the Presidency proper. The local variety of cotton all over Sind, except in the Upper Sind Frontier, is identical with that described previously under the name Jari, which here, however, under the influence of irrigation, yields five to 10 times as much per acre. It might be argued that, even under the inundation canals, since the quantity of water available is at least equal to that falling as rain in the Surtee Broach tract, the superior cotton of the latter tract might be grown in place of the inferior Jari. Here, however, the question of temperature comes in, and where the cotton cannot be sown before June, it is necessary to grow an early ripening variety, because frost generally occurs in January. Jari ripens in five months and Broach in eight, and it is, therefore, uncertain whether Broach would mature on inundation canals in Sind.

What is required, therefore, for a radical improvement of the cotton in Sind is an improvement in the irrigation.

Rohri Canal and Sukkur Barrage.

For the last 50 years various irrigation schemes for this district have been proposed for the purpose of increasing the cultivable area of this fertile plain, and just now a a very large and complicated project for the construction of a canal from Rohri to Hyderabad and a barrage at Sukkur is under examination by the Inspector General of Irrigation. *The cotton industry would be well advised to see that this or another scheme is carried out in the near future, as through it a considerably increased area for cotton cultivation will be thrown open.* When the barrage at Sukkur and the canals are constructed, which is such a gigantic work that it would take about 10 years, all the land in Sind, except the desert and part of the alluvial sand in the south, will have a perennial supply of water.

The perennial Jamrao Canal feeds 700,000 acres with water, and the Sukkur project would supply 2,700,000 acres. The Indus River contains ample water to supply all the proposed irrigation schemes.

Sind has altogether an area of 30 million acres, half of which is unsuitable for irrigation and half is an alluvial soil like the Mississippi and and Nile Deltas. The population of Sind is only 3,500,000, but experience has proved that generally a large influx of people takes place as soon as irrigation works have been completed, and, therefore, the present scarcity of population need not cause any great anxiety.

Unfortunately, the natives of Sind are careless in their methods of cultivation.

The land is owned almost exclusively by "Jogidars," landowners who have received their possessions for services rendered to the Government, and they pay now merely an annual land occupation tax of about 1 rupee per acre. "Zemindars" (large landowners) pay an annual assessment of from 2 to 4 rupees, inclusive of water supply.

Agriculture in Sind is at present dependent on the following means of water supply :—

1. Rain, falling over an area of 10,000,000 acres, mostly desert land, of which only a small proportion is cultivated.
2. Kharif (hot weather). Rice flow, *i.e.*, plenty of water obtainable from river (Indus) and canals for rice cultivation.
3. Kharif Lift. Water must be lifted by instruments, such as the Persian wheels. This land is suitable for cotton.
4. Jamrao Canal. This is a perennial canal irrigating land, suitable for cotton.
5. Bosi. Land flooded once or twice during hot weather and cropped during cold weather. Cotton could be grown on the land.
6. Kucha. Flooded silt land, alluvial soil, no cotton at present.

Fallow Land.

The striking feature of Sind agriculture is that the native cultivates only one-third or one-fourth, or even one-fifth of the land he possesses in one year. The remainder is allowed to lie fallow; fields are left entirely untouched for years, and on riding through the district one sees much more fallow than cultivated land. Whilst these fields lie idle all kinds of bushes grow. The cotton sticks are left standing for years, and I am convinced they harbour insects. I saw a great number of white ants in these fallow fields. The Government does not allow the land to lie idle longer than five years, and if the fields are then not cultivated the assessment is charged also on the non-cultivated land, and if not paid the land is taken away. In Egypt a decree exists, according to which, by December 31st in

A FALLOW COTTON FIELD IN SIND.

(Notice the dried-up cotton sticks and the small shrubs.—Only once in three or even five years is a field cultivated.)

each year, all the roots and cotton sticks must be pulled up and taken from the fields, as it has been proved that insects increase if the sticks are left in the field.

In view of this custom of allowing the fields to lie idle for so long a time, the Jamrao Canal was constructed to supply sufficient water only for one-third of the available land. The supply is not sufficient to irrigate all the rich lands, and it is only by the construction of the Rhori Canal that the whole area can be put under cultivation.

Labour is generally provided by the tenants' family, but in case of help being required no actual money is paid. The pickers receive one-tenth of the cotton they have gathered in lieu of wages.

The yield of Sind cotton in the fields of the ordinary cultivator is from 4 to 5 maunds of 81lbs. seed-cotton per acre, about 31 to 34 per cent. being fibre.

Rotations of crop are not practised in Sind in connection with cotton. As it is the custom after a cotton crop to leave the land fallow for a number of years, it is not considered necessary to rotate the crops. It would be very much to the advantage of the cultivator to grow pulse crops instead of leaving the land bare, as rotations are the most powerful means of improving the soil.

Agricultural Implements.

The *implements* used in general practice are the plough, leveller, and a log of wood for pressing in the seed and breaking the clods. For irrigation land it is essential that its surface should be level. It is a source of great waste of water when the land is uneven. It also tends to accumulate the salt at one end of the field. It is important to have the division plots small, not over 1 acre, but better half an acre, and on no account should the water from the divisions be allowed to flow into the next. At the Government Farm at Mirpurkhas an improved one-handled wooden plough and a leveller (Cassabiah) are being made and sold at cost price, viz., 5 and 7 rupees respectively. The original Sindhi plough has only a small wooden peg, which enters the soil and scrapes it rather than ploughs it.

Method of Cultivation.

The method of sowing after irrigation is simply by scattering seed broadcast, then ploughing it in and running the wooden log over. Sowing the seed in straight lines is not said to be possible in Sind. In the cultivation and preparation of the land the chief things to note are the necessity of thorough and deep ploughing and the getting rid of all weeds and jungle. It is an excellent practice to keep fallow land well ploughed. The Punjabi Colonists on the Jamrao Canal know this, and often plough five or six times during the hot weather the land which is going to grow wheat; in consequence they have the best wheat crops on the Jâmrao.

Alkali is found all over Sind, and where it is very prominent it is impossible for ordinary plants to live. It occurs in small patches and also in large areas, and if only present in moderate quantities, ordinary crops can be cultivated, but they require much water, and the yield is much lessened. When alkali land can be flooded from an inundation canal, coarse red rice can be cultivated. If this be continued for several years the alkali will gradually be washed down into the sub-soil. To do this, however, the land must be level, and each division must be watered direct from the water course, and the water must not be allowed to flow from one division to another. Otherwise the alkali is simply accumulated in patches at the ends of the plots. Alkali can only be got rid of by means of water, and rice properly cultivated is the easiest means of effecting this.

Land Tenure.

In ordinary circumstances the owner of the land does not cultivate it himself, and seldom does he take any interest in it. Each year "haries" or tenants are engaged by the owner. He pays them in advance or from "Takavi," often about 50 rupees for one family, who will cultivate 10 acres. The "takavi" is returned in kind at harvest. On flow land the rent returnable to "Zemindars" is often one-half the produce; the latter pays the Government assessment or land tax. This is the "butai" system. On lift land the "butai" may be one-third to the "Zemindar" and two-thirds to the "Hari."

The number of crops in Sind is extremely limited. Rice is the most important; "jowar" and "bajri" come next, and wheat and cotton, with a small amount of oil seeds, chiefly jambo or rape. The other crops only form a very small proportion of the total.

Before much improvement can be effected in Sind agriculture, it is necessary to persuade the average "Zemindar" to take more interest in his land, and not to leave everything to the annual "Hari" or tenant. Then the next important improvement is the introduction of pulse crops to take the place of some of the bare fallows, as they not only give valuable seed, but supply fodder for the cattle and improve the fertility of the land.

Landowners let out the land in lots of about 20 acres, and share the crop with the tenants, consequently they may dictate to them what crops they must grow. This is a very important factor. As the Deputy Director is held in high esteem by the landowners, they are generally willing to follow any of his recommendations. In the North of Sind the tenants occupy the land for several years, but in the South of Sind they are of a nomadic type, and often change every year.

Kinds of Cotton Grown.

The ordinary local cotton is a very low class. It has only ⅜in. to ½in. staple, and the yield is 7 maunds of 81lbs. per acre under good local cultivation, for which the average price recently has been 6 rupees per "maund."

For a number of years both "Afifi" and "Abassi" Egyptian cottons have been grown. Altogether 6,000 acres have been under cultivation with Egyptian cotton in Sind. The produce was collected by the cultivators and sent in different lots to the Mirpukhas Government Farm, where it was sold by auction. It is quite evident that there were bound to be considerable variations in the quality, cleanness, and value of the different lots, but nevertheless for the first few years fair prices were obtained. The buyers were millowners from Ahmedabad and Bombay, and the exporters from Karachi and Bombay. Several of the millowners who were in the habit of sending buyers were accustomed to use imported Egyptian cotton, but they soon stopped attending these auction sales. They complained that they could not get a fixed grade, whilst, when buying Egyptian cotton in Alexandria or Liverpool they got a certain grade which was uniform and could be depended upon to spin certain counts. For the purchase of Sind Egyptian cotton they had to send their agents on a long journey to Mirpukhas at a time of the year when malaria fever was very prevalent, and these agents, not speaking the Sind language, were a further disadvantage. To buy any quantity, they had to bid for a number of small lots, some of which were dirty and stained, whilst others were good. The gins in Sind are only suitable for short staple cotton, and as they were well engaged on this kind the buyers had great difficulty in getting their cotton ginned at local ginning factories. There does not, therefore, seem to be any possibility of the Indian millowners ever purchasing their Egyptian cotton direct from the cultivator, unless they could be assured that they would have considerable quantities of baled and graded cotton. The cotton broker is undoubtedly an essential link between the cultivator and the spinner. Egyptian cotton was perfectly new to the exporting firms, and the "Abassi" produced in Sind was certainly not to be compared with the Egyptian product. The "Afifi" quality, however, was strong and useful. If it had been cleaned properly, ginned, and baled it would certainly have sold at the rates of "fully good fair Egyptian brown." Both "Abassi" and Afifi cotton shipped were never properly cleaned and were full of dirt and pieces of leaf. Experiments have proved that, here as well as in Egypt, "Afifi" is a hardier cotton than "Abassi." The Deputy Director, Mr. G. S. Henderson, who has had considerable experience of farming in Egypt, is of opinion that, provided the cultivator gets 12 rupees per maund of 81 lbs. for seed-Afifi, it will be more profitable to him than cultivating Sind-cotton. "Afifi" produces in Sind about 5 maunds per acre, whilst the yield of Sind-cotton might average 7 maunds at 6 rupees.

During the last two years the supply of water in the Jamrao Canal has been very short, and the cultivators, not being able to obtain sufficient water for the growing of Egyptian cotton, had to be released from the undertaking, which they had given when entering into possession of the land, to grow a certain proportion under Egyptian cotton. Until the Sukkur Barrage and the Rohri Canals are completed, it will be impossible, in view of the shortage of water in the canals, to grow Egyptian cotton on an extensive scale.

Fairly large trials have been made with a good class of *American Upland cotton.* It has the advantage of a short growing period, shorter than Sind-cotton, and consequently it can be grown along inundation canals. There is a very large tract where it can be cultivated. It is a hardy plant, but it is easily affected by salt in the soil, and suffers considerably from white ants. During the past year some good yields were obtained by farmers, and in many cases it produced as much seed-cotton as the neighbouring plots of Sind-cotton. The following is an expression of opinion from a letter addressed by Messrs. Gaddum & Co., Ltd., Karachi, to the Deputy Director of Agriculture at Mirpukhas, as to the value of this American cotton grown in Sind :—

"We have been requested to write to you by Mr. Arno Schmidt, the Secretary of the International Federation of Master Cotton Spinners, in reference to growing American seed-cotton in Sind.

"We are greatly in favour of this, and have seen samples of Kapas (seed-cotton) shown to us by Mr. Schmidt, and think the cotton would compare very favourably with Middling American cottons, and would fetch at ordinary times at least 1d. to 1½d. per pound more than ordinary Sind cotton in Europe. It is better staple than the American seed-cotton grown in Tinnevelly.

"We think a good market could be made for this cotton, and any exporters would buy it readily at profitable rates to producers, especially if it were obtainable in fairly large quantities and if there existed some certainty of it being free from ordinary Sind cotton.

"We shall be very pleased if you can put us in the way of purchasing some of this cotton, even if only 10 bales, which we would forward to our Manchester House and get their views as to what prices it would bring in Lancashire.

"Of course, a season like the present one is most difficult, as the price at present of ordinary Sind cotton is the same as Middling American; in other words, the price of East Indian cotton is not on a parity with American, and should be nearly 1d. per pound lower.

"The serious difficulty experienced by us in dealing with growers of American seed-cotton has been that we have been offered their cotton on a sample, and when bulk has been inspected it has always had a percentage of inferior (ordinary) cotton mixed with it. If growers could be persuaded not to do this, and buyers could be sure of obtaining pure American seed-cotton unmixed with lower kinds, it would be a help to fixing a standard rate compared with ordinary cotton.

"In Broach, where the class of cotton is high and the staple good, the natives bring large quantities of inferior Kapas in from other districts and mix it, and thus make good profits, also the seed ginned from this cotton deteriorates yearly, and gradually the original pure Broach cotton is disappearing.

"If this is done with American seed-cotton it will never, in our opinion, be a success, and prices that would be profitable to dealers would never be paid. We learnt that Messrs. Tata, of Bombay, are buying the cotton grown on the experimental farms at Lyallpur at

6 rupees per maund above the rate for ordinary cotton on the condition that the cotton is not mixed, &c.

"We have had some experience of American seed-cotton in the Tinnevelly district, where it is increasing rapidly and is readily bought by mills and exporters at evidently profitable rates to growers, as it is yearly increasing.

"This cotton is very well liked by spinners at home, and commands 1d. per pound more in price than the ordinary Tinnevelly cotton.

"The amount of this kind of cotton has been so small up to now in any other district except Tinnevelly that it has hardly been worth exporters' while to bother about it. However, with reasonable prospects of the quantity increasing and quality being kept up, we are quite convinced that a good business might be done at rates which would compare favourably with ordinary Sind cotton from the cultivators' point of view.

"We shall be glad at any time to do anything in our power to help you in this matter or to hear from you at any time."

This letter is also interesting in so far as it shows that it is very difficult, if not impossible, to rely upon an Indian cultivator supplying the genuine article; *he evidently cannot withstand the temptation of mixing inferior cotton with superior ones.*

As the Deputy Director thought that he would be able to persuade the "Zemindars" to plant American cotton-seed where they had previously grown Sindhi cotton, and as there is apparently no further attention by the cultivators required for the growing of American cotton, I discussed, on his suggestion, the question of substituting American cotton for Sind cotton with the Commissioner of Sind, and the final outcome of my interview with him was that the Government ordered 40 tons of American cotton seed (Triumph) from the British Cotton Growing Association.

At present Sind produces some 170,000 bales of Sind-cotton, and there is every possibility of the cultivation of American cotton being taken up in place of it. Egyptian cotton requires 6 to 8 weeks' earlier sowing than American cotton and necessitates 22 waterings, whilst 12 to 13 waterings would be quite ample for American cotton.

Government Farm at Mirpukhas.

The management is in the excellent hands of the Deputy Director of Agriculture, *Mr. G. S. Henderson,* who is very practical in all that he undertakes. From what I could see the large landowners readily take up any suggestions he makes.

The following statement will be of interest :—

No. of Plot.	Crop.	Previous cropping and cultivation.	No. of watering	Date of sowing.	Date of last watering.	Total Canal watering in cubic feet per acre.	Total Canal watering in inches.	Total rainfall in inches.	Produce in lbs. per acre.	Remarks.
1	2	3	4	5	6	7	8	9	10	11
C. 4	Egyptian Cotton Abassi.	Berseem in Rabi, 1909. Twice ploughed, sammared and ridged. Seed dibbled on ridges.	15	15th April, 1910	24th October, 1910.	114,207	31⅓	7·88	254 Seed Cotton ..	This crop is sown on ridges and the first waterings are given along the bottom of the farrows. No berseem sown in Rabi.
C. 5	Sind Cotton ..	Berseem in Rabi, 1909. Ploughed four times, and seed sown after the last plough and sammared.	7	19th May, 1910	23rd October, 1910.	72,389	20	7·88	1,304 do. ..	No berseem sown in Rabi.
C. 6	American Cotton Boyd Prolific.	Berseem in Rabi, 1909. Twice ploughed and seed sown after the plough and sammared.	12	24th May, 1910	6th December, 1910.	129,988	35	7·88	330 do. ..	Berseem sown broad cast on 25th September, 1910. Four last waterings for berseem.
C 7	Egyptian Cotton Mit Afifi.	Berseem in Rabi, 1909. Twice ploughed and sammared and ridged. Seed dibbled on ridges.	20	15th April, 1910	7th December, 1910.	168,514	46¼	7·88	342 do. ..	Berseem sown. Four last waterings for berseem.
D. 6	Sholapuri Jowar	Berseem in Rabi, 1909. Twice ploughed and seed broad casted and then sammared.	9	27th May, 1910	15th November, 1910.	98,366	27	7·88	960lbs. Grain and 7,500lbs. Fodder.	This crop is much later in ripening than local Sindhi jowar.
D. 7	Awned Bajri ..	Berseem in Rabi, 1909. Twice ploughed and seed broad casted.	6	18th May, 1910	28th September, 1910.	61,960	17	4·88	60lbs. Grain and 1,000lbs. Fodder.	This crop was a failure owing to insufficient watering.

NOTE.—A preliminary watering of 15,000 cubic feet per acre given to each plot to soften ground for cultural operations.

At *Daulatpur* Mr. Henderson has reclaimed 400 acres of alkali land on the Egyptian method of land reclamation; on this tract he is growing at present cotton and the Egyptian berseem (clover). The latter is entirely a new crop for India, and in consequence of the success attained in Sind with this leguminous plant, experiments are being undertaken in practically all the Provinces of India. Berseem is an excellent fodder, and at the same time gives back nitrogen to the soil. It is probably due to this crop that the Egyptian soil keeps so fertile. The 400 acres reclaimed will serve as a seed farm.

Ginning Factories

The gins are nearly all Platts' roller gins; they are largely owned by European export houses. The cotton arrives in farmers' bales, on the backs of camels, or on carts, at the gins, where it is ginned and put first into loose bales; after a few days these are hydraulically pressed in the same establishment. It seems to me a waste of time and wages to put cotton provisionally into bales. The only explanation for this twice pressing was that the hydraulic press worked so quickly that the gins could not deliver sufficient cotton to keep it employed all the week, consequently they had to work up a stock of ginned cotton, which they put into loose bales. When a sufficient quantity of these was ready, the hydraulic press was started. At none of the ginneries are there pneumatic suction pipes or automatic feeding appliances. The wages paid at the gins are 6d. for men for 14 hours. The average turn-out per press is 300 bales of 400lbs. in 10 hours. 100 bales take up 20 tons measurement.

Buying Agency.

In view of the introduction of American cotton into Sind on a pretty large scale it might be advisable to make arrangements with one of the existing firms of exporters of cotton to guarantee through them to the farmer a fixed price above either the local cotton grown or a fixed price on the basis of middling American cotton in Liverpool. The Deputy Director thought that the farmers ought to be guaranteed an increase in price of 20 per cent. over that of Sind-cotton, which is not half an inch in staple. It might be found advisable to set up a saw-ginning factory for the American cotton if the native can be taught to handle the saw-gins. I am told roller-gins, if run slowly, gin American cotton even better than saw-gins, as the fibre is not so much damaged by the rollers and knife, but, of course, the saw-gins turn out more work.*

New Land.

When the land through which the proposed Rohri Canal will pass is being opened up it will be advisable for the Government to insist upon a certain proportion of it being cultivated under cotton *in accordance with the instructions of the Department of Agriculture.* In this manner the Government would create free of charge a number of demonstration farms, and the cotton industry would be assured of an increased area, producing a good quality of cotton. It is beyond doubt that the large portions of land through which these canals will

*I hear that the spinners of Bombay are in treaty with the Government as regards the establishment of a buying and ginning centre in Sind.

run are highly suitable for the cultivation of cotton, and it should be no hardship for the cultivators to accept such a stipulation. A similar stipulation was willingly agreed to by the colonists along the Jamrao Canal with regard to the growing of Egyptian cotton, and in the Punjab, along the Chenab Canal, the Government insists upon the rearing of horses, &c., for the army, by the farmers who have received new land along the canal.

I am convinced, provided the Department of Agriculture will see that the cotton produced by the 40 tons of American seed previously referred to, which ought to produce about 3,000 bales, is not mixed with the inferior local cotton, there will be little difficulty in disposing of the crop, as it will be highly suitable for Indian, Japanese, and European millowners.

PUNJAB.

The total area is 89,000 square miles, of which 42,000 are cultivated. The population is 25,000,000.

Cotton is grown on 1,300,000 acres, of which almost a million are irrigated. During the previous season about 270,000 bales of 400lbs. each of cotton have been picked. The rainfall average for the Province is 23½in., ranging from 50in. to 60in. in the Sub-Montane tracts, to 6in. to 7in. only in the Western part of the Punjab.

The great feature of the Punjab as regards agriculture is the following perennial canal system:—

			Acres.
Chenab Canal	irrigating	roughly	2,000,000
Baridoab	,,	,,	1,000,000
Sirhind	,,	,,	1,000,000
Western Jumna	,,	,,	800,000
Jhelum	,,	,,	800,000

The Upper Chenab Canal is under construction. It will irrigate the district of Montgomery, which is without doubt the most suitable cotton-growing district, and several experts expressed the opinion that the land along the Montgomery Canal ought to produce at least 50,000 bales of first-class cotton per year. This Canal will be in working condition by 1914, and the cotton spinners should immediately approach the Government with a view to this new land being given out with the stipulation that a portion of it be grown under cotton in accordance with the instructions of the Department of Agriculture. The Agricultural Department ought to reserve an area of at least 400 acres for a large "nucleus" seed farm.

I was informed that the Government desired to give preference to the cultivation of sugar-cane in this district, but the climatic conditions for its cultivation are not favourable, it being too dry; the land is much more suitable for cotton, and, moreover, it should be taken into consideration that sugar requires five times as much water as cotton. Wheat requires more labour than cotton, a factor which ought to be borne in mind in view of the scarcity of labour that will exist when the new district is being opened up.

I visited *Lyallpur,* the capital of the recently established Chenab Colony. Lyallpur was founded in 1896, and now it is a town with about 18,000 inhabitants. In the early nineties a solitary tree would have been famous as a landmark.

Mr. J. Ramsay Macdonald, M.P., describes the change which has come about in the Chenab Colony excellently in his recent publication, "The Awakening of India." He says: "The land was barren but for useless scrub and for short-lived fodder which sprang up after the rains, and on account of which the land paid a grazing rent of about one penny per acre. Across it roamed primitive nomadic peoples, who subsisted largely on cattle-lifting, and whose ways of life are well shown in a proverb which was current amongst them: '*My child, if you cannot steal, you will die of hunger.*' An escort was required for caravans and cattle droves crossing this territory, and a regular scale of payment for protective services at the rate of 2½ per cent. of the value of the property guarded was accepted. A fee of 10 rupees was paid to the tribesmen to pursue and attempt to recover a stolen camel or buffalo. All that is changed. A canal constructed as an inundation channel in 1887 was made into an irrigation canal, and the country was ready for colonisation at the beginning of 1892. The cattle-lifter is now handling the plough, and is being taught the allurements of the law courts. An area of 3,800 square miles—with another 2,000 within range—of which 3,000 are already allotted to cultivators, has been irrigated. In 1901 83,000 people, drawn from congested districts of the north and north-west, and grouped in 1,418 villages, had settled upon it. They came with all their village communities — washermen, barbers, carpenters, smiths, sweepers—and settled in their new surroundings. Discouraged at first by many circumstances, not the least of which was a virulent outbreak of cholera, but encouraged by a good crop, they took root, and now they tell you merrily of their interesting experiences. 'I came on a camel,' said one of the cultivators to me, 'and now——' He left his sentence to be finished by a significant sweep of his hand across the landscape shaded by trees and rich in growing crops. Railways are running through the district and grain markets have been opened at different centres. The export of wheat from the area was 8,124,607 maunds in 1903, and each acre yields on the average 20 to 30 "maunds." In addition to that, cotton is grown, 567,212 "maunds" having been exported in 1903. The land revenue amounts to one million and a quarter rupees, and the canal dues range between eight and ten million rupees. That is the Government income from the Colony, and it certainly does not represent more than a fair economic rent. Truly we can say this of the place: '*The desert shall rejoice and blossom as the rose.*'"

The people of the Punjab are industrious and pretty good cultivators. They are even taking up ploughing with the steel plough, and reaping machines and other modern agricultural implements are gradually being introduced by the Agricultural Department. The cultivators are eager to take up any recommendation which the Department may make, and the officials recognise that in order to strengthen this confidence it is necessary that only such recommendations be made as experience has proved to be likely of success.

The cotton crop is well liked by the natives because the principal work connected with it falls at a time when no other pressing agricultural work requires their attention.

Land Tenure. The Punjab is a Province of peasant proprietors each owning 4 to 6 acres, but along the canal a holding is about 20 acres.

Kinds of Cotton. The Punjab produces *two very nice indigenous cottons* called "Hansi" and "Multan." They are ⅝in. fully in staple, and yield 7 to 8 maunds of seed cotton per acre. Their average ginning outturn is 33 per cent., but some of the native cottons produce a ⅞in. staple, and the ginning outturn of some cotton round the town of Multan is as high as 40 per cent.

A ginner told me that a good deal of the Punjab native cotton is sold in Europe as Surtee-Broach cotton.

American cotton, from seed supplied by the Dharwar Government farm (where it was introduced some 50 years ago), has been grown along the Chenab Canal for the last seven years, and one might say that since 1908 it has been cultivated on a somewhat extensive scale. There is this year a crop of some 600 bales of this Dharwar-American cotton to be had, 400 bales of which have been sold to a large Ahmedabad spinning mill at the price of "fully good fair American, loco. Ahmedabad."* In former years this American cotton was sold by auction in an unginned condition, and the ginners had paid 2/- per 82lbs. more for it than for the local cotton. The Deputy Director of Agriculture told me that the Agricultural Department had not pushed the general introduction of this American cotton because it had kept improving from year to year, and before persuading the farmers to take up this cotton in place of the local cotton the Department wanted to have a sufficient supply of pure seed. The Department is experimenting also with a variety of Dharwar-American which is earlier maturing. If these experiments are successful it will be a great advantage, as that cotton would not require water at a time when the wheat crop is very much in need of it. Another of the reasons why the Department is not anxious for the introduction of this kind of cotton was that the officials did not consider that the farmer obtained sufficient remuneration for this improved variety. I am inclined to think that in view of the unclean condition in which the cotton is picked in comparison with American cotton the officials as well as the cultivators over-estimate its value. Some of the exporters assured me that they had offered quite a fair price for this American cotton in previous years; they had, of course, to take into consideration that it was always full of leaves, stalks, &c. These impurities get into the cotton during picking because the plants become very dry and brittle, especially after a frost. It must also be borne in mind that these cottons are not quite as even in staple as cotton from America. The exporters also told me that frequently local cotton seed is sown along with the American seed, which, of course, reduces the value of the latter. Such mixing benefits the

* Cost of transport on American cotton from Liverpool to Ahmedabad is calculated at ·46d. per pound.

farmer if undetected, because the local cotton has a higher ginning outturn, but in a few years the deterioration owing to this mixing will be a very serious factor.

Gins. In some Provinces of India the export firms have their own ginneries, and no doubt when the amount of American cotton grown in the Punjab becomes important enough, one or the other export firms will establish a ginning factory, with saw gins if necessary. At present all the gins are of the roller type. The ginneries of the Punjab are entirely in the hands of native firms, who, I am told, speculate largely in cotton. There is an ample supply of ginneries, and at any time one of these

A farmer's cart in the Punjab taking Seed-Cotton to the Ginnery.

could be hired for the purpose of ginning this American cotton. Such a step would guarantee this cotton being kept pure, and I think the cotton exporters ought to consider it in their own interests to deal in a higher-priced article than the present cotton; their profit would then be correspondingly larger without their work being materially increased.

I met the owners of some of the largest ginning factories in the Punjab. They told me that they fix their price for the local cotton regardless of the length of staple. Their only gauge is the ginning outturn. It is interesting to note that the ginning outturn of the local cotton is now on an average 33 per cent., whilst in 1897 it was only 25 per cent. to 27 per cent. As mentioned before, some of the local cotton round Multan gives a ginning percentage of 40, and the ginners assured me that they keep the seed of this cotton strictly separate and sell it to the farmers for sowing purposes.

Marketing the Cotton.

The cotton is bought outright by the ginner, only in rare cases does he buy direct from the farmer; the latter sells his crop to the "bania" or dealer, who frequently advances money on the produce before it is harvested. The "bania" collects various lots and sells them to the ginner. The cotton exporter buys the cotton from the latter. Ginners here do not gin on commission. After the cotton has been ginned it is put up in temporary bales called "boras," and then pressed again for transport. The same is done in Sind. Everywhere an enormous waste of labour is evident. I was pleased, however, that one ginner had a strong desire to reduce his wages bill. He was experimenting with a self-feeding apparatus which he had constructed for the gins, and when I spoke to him about the pneumatic transmitters of cotton as used in America he asked for full particulars. Owing to the enormous irrigation works which are being carried on at present in the Punjab (there are some 60,000 men engaged in their construction), labour has become somewhat scarce and the wages for the men in the ginnery have gone up from 4d. a day in 1907 to 12d. at the present time. There is an amalgamation of ginners in Lyallpur, all pooling the profits of ginning and baling.

Methods of Cultivation.

The soil is generally either sandy or alluvial. The cultivation of cotton depends largely on the preceding crop; for example, when following sugar cane or Toria (Brassica campestris), the land is ploughed as many times as possible in the winter and irrigated for the sowing in April. The seed is scattered broadcast after the ploughing at a rate of 8lbs. or 10lbs. per acre, then the plough and the "sohaga" (plough-harrow) are passed over. When cotton follows wheat there is very little time for preparing the soil for the sowing. In well-tracts the land is generally manured for cotton when it follows wheat. Sowing by drills or on ridges is scarcely known, and even sowing behind a plough in lines is carried on in a few places only. Intercultivation with a hand-hoe or a country plough is practised only once.

The Agricultural Department has demonstrated the advisability of sowing in lines and intercultivating with a hand-hoe or a plough after the first, third, or fourth irrigations. In the Lyallpur district six to seven waterings are given. Sowing in drills on the flat has given quite as good results as sowing on ridges, and therefore the latter system has been definitely abandoned by the Department of Agriculture. When seed has been sown on ridges more water is required in the field. Although the people sow broadcast, some run the native plough in between the plants, tearing up here and there a few of them.

Rotation of Crops.

A good rotation, which is, however, not generally recognised, is wheat, oil seeds, cotton, wheat, &c. Singhi (Melilotus parviflores) is a leguminous crop, and is sown sometimes amongst the cotton in a similar way to "Berseem" (clover) in Egypt.

The land in the Punjab may be classed as growing :—

50 per cent. Wheat.
25 per cent. Toria (a rape seed [brassica campestris]).
16 per cent. Cotton.
9 per cent. Fodder (jowar, millet, &c.).

Agricultural Labour.

As each tenant farms his own land, outside labour is rarely required. During the picking season a few women are employed who receive $\frac{1}{6}$ or $\frac{1}{10}$ of the cotton they pick in lieu of wages. The yield per acre in the rainy tracts is 4½ maunds, and in canal tracts 6 maunds per acre. There are six to ten pickings in one season.

The following statement was given to me by a cultivator :—

First picking, 1 maund of 82lbs. of inferior quality.
Second and third picking, 6 maunds of best quality.
Last picking, 1 maund of inferior quality.
Average, 8 maunds of 82 lbs. seed-cotton.

It is very strange that the first picking in this Province is of inferior quality, whilst in other Provinces it is best of all.

The cotton stalks are cut and used for fuel.

Manure.

Cotton is often manured in well-lands when following wheat, generally about 2 to 3 tons of farm manure are applied. When cotton follows sugar-cane there is no need for manure as sugar cane is heavily manured. On all other lands no manure is used for the cotton crop.

Seed Distribution

Lyallpur Agricultural Station supplies selected seeds of "Hansi" and "Multan" cotton and of Dharwar-American in very small quantities. There is also a seed farm at *Sargodha* which supplies selected seed to the Jhelum Colony. The amount of selected seed supplied in this way is comparatively small. Here again I take the liberty of recommending that the system of seed distribution of the Central Provinces should be followed.

Insect Pests.

The Boll-worm has done considerable damage this season, especially amongst the indigenous cotton; the only remedy applied was the parasite called "Rhogas Lefroyi"; this was discovered by the Entomologist at the Pusa Research Institute, and is called after him. This parasite attacks the worm, lays its eggs in it, and kills it. I was informed that the introduction of this parasite by the Agricultural Department had been of some success, but, unfortunately, through some unexplained reason, the parasites died off in large numbers, probably through an attack from another parasite. One expert said that he would try next season the experiment of passing a rope round the cotton plants and shake them whilst the field is being irrigated; he believes that the worms will fall off through the shaking of the plants and will drown in the water. Experience has shown that when there is a strong wind during the period of irrigation many boll-worms drop off and perish in the water.

Lyallpur Agricultural College.

There is an Agricultural College at Lyallpur, and efforts are made to induce the sons of farmers to study there. So far this aim does not seem to have been achieved, as the last annual report of the College contains the following paragraph: "Most of the men have no object except to win an educational qualification which will secure them ser-

Agricultural College at Lyallpur (Punjab).

Agricultural College at Cawnpore (U.P.)

vice under the Government. The College is not popular with the classes we wish to attract, nor indeed with any class."

The other Agricultural Colleges in India have had similar experience with their students. but an improvement seems to be making itself felt.

In connection with the Agricultural College is a demonstration farm which is well managed by the Professor of Agriculture, *Mr. W. Roberts*. The usual experiments as to manuring, planting, &c., are demonstrated there.

Results at this farm for the past few years have shown that Kidney, Spence, Caravonica Tree cotton, African and Egyptian cottons have been failures, principally owing to the lateness in maturing. In October and November severe frosts occur regularly, the crop must therefore be quite ripe by that time. The best cottons in the Punjab appear to be the Dharwar-American cottons and the indigenous cottons. Six Dharwar-American selections have been up to date handed over to the Professor of Agriculture, Punjab Agricultural College, Lyallpur, for trial on larger areas before finally being recommended to cultivators.

A new Government farm is being laid out by the Deputy Director, *Mr. S. Milligan*, at *Gurdaspur;* its area is 104 acres, but hardly any of it will be utilised for cotton. Mr. Milligan possesses a thorough knowledge of the conditions obtaining in the Punjab, and is a valuable asset to the Department.

Buying Agency.

A buying agency in the Punjab would undoubtedly be a stimulus to the growers to cultivate long staple cotton, but owing to the frequent mixing of various kinds of cotton, none but an old-established firm could protect the interests of the spinners.

UNITED PROVINCES OF AGRA AND OUDH.

These Provinces are divided into the Western district with its centre round *Aligarh,* and the Southern district with *Cawnpore* as its centre.

WESTERN DISTRICT.

The Aligarh farm is under the direct supervision of the Deputy Director, *Dr. A. E. Parr,* who has considerable influence amongst the cultivators.

The cotton area of the United Provinces is normally 1,500,000 acres, yielding about 350,000 bales, equal to ¼ bale per acre, say 100lbs. The low yield per acre may be partially accounted for by the fact that cotton is frequently sown with other products such as " Bhindi " (lady's finger).

Water Supply.

The Western part of the United Provinces is well supplied with perennial irrigation from the Ganges and the Jumna. The district thus irrigated forms the most important portion of the cotton growing area of the United Provinces. In normal years 25 to 30 per cent. of the cotton in this district is irrigated, whilst the remainder is grown on natural rainfall. A new irrigation canal, the "Hathras" Canal, has just been opened; it irrigates the district where cotton has already been grown under natural rainfall, but there will probably be an increased yield per acre in consequence of the irrigation.

Land Tenure. There are small holders of land of, say, 10 acres who cultivate their holdings themselves. There are also large landowners who have tenants who must be divided into two classes, viz. :—

(*a*) Permanent right tenants,
(*b*) Tenants at will;

the latter can be ejected at any time, but the former are tenants for life.

The landlord pays half of the rent he receives to the Government as assessment; the rent varies from Rs. 3 to 3·12·0. per acre; the water used for the canals is paid for separately, the rate for cotton is about Rs. 2. 8. 0. per acre. Each kind of crop has a different water-tax.

The soil is loamy.

Kinds of Cotton. The variety grown is ordinary Bengal (G. neglectum); it has an average staple of ⅝in.; its value is almost entirely dependent upon the ginning outturn, the colour affects it also slightly. The ginning outturn of the ordinary local cotton is about 33 per cent. fibre, but Dr. Parr has 500 acres under cultivation of an improved indigenous kind that yields 39 per cent. fibre. The Agricultural Department is using every effort to improve this kind, and next year there will be some 2,500 acres of this cotton grown under the Department's supervision. This cotton is being introduced simply on account of the high ginning out-turn, which makes its cultivation to the farmer much more lucrative than that of American cotton. The staple of the new variety is ½in., and the yield 10 maunds of 82lbs. on good soil.

Until two years ago some nice *American* cotton of 1in. staple was grown in the district of Aligarh and sold at the same price as that ruling for American middling. In spite of the fair price paid by a Calcutta spinning mill, the cultivation of American cotton was not remunerative to the farmer. The difference in price between American and local East Indian cotton did not prove sufficiently high. The yield per acre was not so great for American cotton as that of the indigenous cotton, and the ginning outturn was also less. The American cotton was grown round separate villages and had to be collected, causing some extra expense. A spinner who had used that cotton expressed to me his high satisfaction with its quality. The Agricultural Department and the native, after fully proving the reduced profit derived from the cultivation of this exotic kind, have definitely given up the idea of growing American cotton and are concentrating their attention on introducing the high yielding indigenous kind mentioned before, and I certainly consider that their action is a right one.

Cultivation. The sowing season is in May on irrigated land, and in June with a rainfall on unirrigated land; the soil is extremely hard at this time of the year, in fact it would be impossible for the steel plough to enter it, therefore the cultivator floods his field to soften the ground, allows it to dry sufficiently in order to permit the wooden native plough to enter the soil. After watering the field he sows the seed broadcast, then ploughs it in and rolls it, as is done in the Punjab; watering and hand-weeding are carefully performed. It is the general opinion of the cultivator that too much preparation of the soil is no advantage as regards the yield of the crop, and therefore he leaves his field

Ginning Cotton by hand.
(Churka)

fallow during the winter season, during which time the roots and short stalks of the previous crop are left in the ground. The soil even at the beginning of winter is so hard that one cannot pull up the roots.

Many cultivators in the district gin sufficient cotton with a native hand-gin, "Churka," to enable them to sow their fields with the seed thus obtained. This is said to be an advantage, as the power gins often cut the seed and thus destroy its germinating power.

Picking begins in October and lasts until the end of December; the first and last pickings are considered inferior in quality and yield to the middle pickings.

After the picking has been finished the cattle are allowed to graze on the cotton fields.

Ginneries.

The ginneries are mostly in the hands of native firms; they are all roller gins, single and double action. As the cotton is picked in a dirty condition it is customary in practically all the Provinces to pass the cotton through an opener before ginning it. *In this district proper export bales are pressed at once, i.e.,* without first making the loose bales as is the custom in Sind and the Punjab. Ginning factories work, generally, three days, and the cotton ginned during that time is pressed on the fourth day. To a fairly large extent the ginners buy the cotton from the "bania," but those who gin on commission charge 7d. per 82lbs. seed-cotton, and about Rs. 3 per bale for pressing. The wages of the men at the press are 6d., those of the women at the gins 4d.

Manure.

During the dry season, October to May, the cattle manure is made into cakes, dried in the sun and afterwards used for fuel, but during the remaining few months this is impossible owing to the rains. During that short time the manure is collected into heaps and used for the preparation of maize and sugar-cane soils. No manure is used for preparing the cotton soil, which benefits solely from the residue of manure that was given to the preceding crop.

Rotation of Crops.

The following may be considered as representative on irrigated land; it has the disadvantage, however, of there being too few leguminous crops :—

Wheat, 6 months.
Cotton, 8 months.
Barley and peas (mixed), 4 months.
Maize, wheat, &c., 6 months.

On unirrigated land cotton, jowar (millet), and Raha (a kind of pea), are often grown mixed.

Insects.

The Boll-worm did considerable damage last season; so far no remedial measures have proved of value. The cotton sticks are cut off for fuel, but the roots remain in the soil; perhaps this is one of the causes of the prevalence of boll worm.

Probable Extension.

If cotton remains at the present high level of prices the area under cultivation will increase at the expense of other crops, otherwise there is not much probability of extension. The yield per acre can, however, be materially increased through the introduction of cotton which gives a high ginning out-turn, and this has been done in some cases. A further increase must be expected from the gradual though slow introduction of improved methods of cultivation.

If the rains had not failed last season at the time of sowing there would have been an increase of some 25 per cent. on the acreage under cotton.

The cultivators in this district generally are ready to take up improved varieties of new seeds, and I was told that the native cultivators are no more conservative in the methods than are the English farmers.

CAWNPORE DISTRICT.

Cawnpore Government Farm.

In the report on my first visit to India I criticised somewhat unfavourably the conditions of cotton demonstration work on the Cawnpore agricultural farm. I was sorry to see on my return that no improvement in this respect had taken place. In justification of the Deputy Director who has charge of this farm I must say that he has been absent for a year and a half on special duty in connection with the Allahabad Exhibition. It was most disheartening to find in such a large cotton-producing area that the Government farm should devote only two acres out of 80 to cotton growing experiments, and some of these were very neglected. I was told that as regards the yield of some of these experimental crops it was impossible to arrive at any definite conclusion owing to the mixture of varieties grown in the plots. The experiments which I saw were certainly not encouraging, and would have acted as a deterrent to any farmer visiting the Government farm.

I complained about the lack of demonstration work as regards cotton on this farm to the officiating Inspector-General of Agriculture, and at the same time I urged the Cawnpore millowners to pass the following resolution :—

> "Whilst *recognising the usefulness of the botanical research work at Cawnpore,* this meeting of Cotton Millowners is of opinion that the Department of Agriculture in the United Provinces should establish seed farms on the lines of those instituted by the Central Provinces Department of Agriculture, which have been an unqualified success, as it is of opinion that only by such a system of seed farms distributed all over the Provinces can suitable strains of cotton be kept pure. Such seed farms are in addition most valuable for purposes of practical demonstration and can be worked, if properly managed, free of cost to Government."

I am pleased to say that I have received the following communication from the officiating Inspector-General :—

> "In continuation of my letter, No. C/417, of 7th January, 1912, addressed C/o Bengal Chamber of Commerce, Calcutta, I have the honour to say that I have been in correspondence with the Director of Agriculture, United Provinces, and I am pleased to inform you that he has taken measures for the improvement of cotton at Cawnpore and other parts of the United Provinces on a more extensive scale than hitherto, and on the lines already so successfully being carried out in the Central Provinces and Madras. I trust this information will dispel any anxiety you may have felt in regard to the treatment of this crop in the United Provinces."

Sowing in the Cawnpore tract begins towards the end of May on irrigated land, otherwise the farmer waits for the monsoon, which generally arrives on the 15th June. As the monsoon was late last season, the area under cotton this year is greatly reduced. Picking begins on the 1st October.

Botanical Research Work.

Excellent work is being carried on at this farm with regard to botanical research by *Mr. H. Martin Leake, M.A.* Research work naturally takes up a number of years before results of much practical value are attained, but I am inclined to think, from what I have seen, that Mr. Leake has arrived at a stage when his several years of labour will prove of real value to the cotton grower. He has obtained, through crossing, a number of varieties which he intends to grow this season under field cultivation, and for this purpose a seed farm of 211 acres has recently been acquired in the neighbourhood of Aligarh. In explanation of his work the following notes may be of interest :—

During the last ten years science has made considerable progress in the field of plant-breeding, and the impetus which has been given in this direction and to what is now generally known as the Science of Genetics, dates from the rediscovery of Mendel's work. The fundamental idea of this new line of work is that the form of a plant is decided by the presence or absence of definite units or characters. Each such character (except in a few cases where "coupling" between characters occurs) behaves independently and must be considered separately.

In hybridization work, when one plant possessing a particular character is crossed by another lacking that character, there will appear in the second generation plants, some of which will possess, and some lack, that character, and from these it is possible to breed with confidence two pure races which will remain pure—one possessing and the other lacking the character in question. Now suppose there are two plants, one possessing a desirable character lacking in the second, while the second possesses a desirable character absent in the first; in the second generation of the cross between these two, (in the absence of "coupling") four types of plants will be found. Two of these will possess one of the desirable characters and lack the other—these are the two parental forms. The other two are new types, and of these one will possess both desirable characters while the other will lack both. It will also be possible to raise all four types obtained from the cross in a pure condition.

Such, in its simplest form, is the method of improving races of economic plants which recent discovery has rendered possible. As applied to cotton it will be understood that, given, for instance, a long stapled race but late flowering and a short stapled race which is early flowering, it is possible to isolate a pure long stapled early-flowering race. It is not meant to convey the idea that the process is in all cases as simple as above stated (difficulty arises in determining what actually constitutes a unit character), but, in the absence of "coupling"—and it may be noted that "coupling" has not been found to occur in any of the essential characters of the cotton plant—it is possible to isolate races possessing a series of desirable characters such as is possessed by no race at the present time. Further, a race so produced will prove as constant as any of the races now found in cultivation.

Mr. Leake has crossed some of his selected strains with a red flower, because he will then be able to distinguish easily when a cultivator has mixed the seed with other kinds, as the cotton generally grown in the United Provinces has a yellow flower.

BURMA.

The following report has been received from the Director of Agriculture, Burma :—

Kinds of Cotton Grown.	Length of Staple.	Approximate quantity grown.
I.—*Wa-gale* (White) .. Wa-pyu (White) .. Gossypium neglectum, Var. vera, sub-var : Burmanica (Annual).	½" to ¾"	This is the commonest variety grown ; it is cultivated in almost every district of dry Central Burma and supplies practically all the staple of commerce. Average about 180,000 acres.
II. *Wa-ni* (Khaki-coloured). G. neglectum, var-vera, sub-var : Kokatio (Annual).	about ¾"	(Sparingly cultivated, chiefly for local consumption. Of no commercial importance.
III. *Wa-gyi* (White). G. obtusifolium, var : Nanking (Perennial tree cotton).	Said to be slightly longer than that of I.	(Commonly grown in Myingyan, Thayetmyo and Minbu). The area under this variety cannot be separately calculated : it is included in No. 1.
IV. Shan Cotton (Khaki-coloured). G. neglectum (Annual).	Short.	Not known, but small. (Said to be grown throughout the Shan States), and used for local manufacture. Little importance commercially.
V. Chin Cotton (Annual).	Short	Small (Chin Hills) for local consumption.
VI. Thinbaw-Wa (the Pernambuco, Chain or Kidney Cotton) G. brasiliense (Perennial tree cotton with white lint).	1·5" (Long, silky, and fairly strong).	Up till a short time ago only scattered trees of this variety were found. It is now being tried on a commercial scale in the Amherst district ; but no results are as yet available.

The final forecast of the cotton crop for Burma for 1911-12 gives 183,075 acres under cotton with an estimated yield of cleaned cotton of 34,000 bales of 400lbs. each. This return refers to the 11 districts in which cotton is of commercial importance. The remaining area is about 1,500 acres ; produce locally utilised.

Soil. "From the richest loam to the poorest up-land." The Burman will *not* grow cotton on land which is suitable for paddy (*rice*) ; so that the chances of its being grown on irrigated land are small.

On *Yas* and Kaing lands.

On poorer soil than is required for sessamum (in Shwebo); medium cotton soil (in Sagaing); on the poorest of cultivated soils (in Sagaing); good to medium soils (in the Myingyan-Meiktila-Sagaing area); also on red marly soils full of pebbles (in the above area); from stiff clays to the poorest stony sands (in Myingyan).

The soils in Myingyan vary from stiff clays (*e.g.*, black cotton soil) to the poorest stony sands. But black cotton soils are *not* the favourite soils for cotton cultivation in Burma. The best cotton soil in Myingyan is a rich silt which forms on the lowest ground in parts of the district.

Method of Cultivation.

In Thayetmyo (one of the largest cotton growing districts) cotton is sown, mixed with other crops, in *yas*, broadcast. The crops with which it is mixed are paddy and sessamum. Two weedings are made—one before and one after the mixed crop is reaped. The cultivation is generally of the roughest description. In Magwe, it is sown as a mixed crop with sessamum or Lu (Panicum miliare). In Shwebo it is sown in rotation with sessamum and pyaung (Sorghum vulgare) or on fields that have already produced a crop or two of sessamum. In Sagaing it is rotated with pyaung, sessamum, and fallows, or the land after cotton is fallowed for a number of years and then sown with sessamum. *Wa-pyu or Wa-gale* is usually sown in May or early June and plucked at the beginning of November. The land is occasionally manured with cattle dung, if available, and harrowed once before the rains break. Ploughing may or may not be done subsequently, the requisite tilth being obtained by the use of the harrow alone. The seed is sown broadcast at the rate of 1½ basket (bushel) of ginned seed per acre; weeding is invariably done by means of a small hand spade. After plucking, the cotton is dried in the sun and carried in carts to the mills. *Wa-gyi* (in Myingyan) is a large tree cotton which is but occasionally cultivated or grown in gardens.

Method of cultivation (in Myingyan): Seed sown, after harrowing, at the rate of four baskets per acre, and covered with the 3-toothed harrow. When about 10 inches high the crop is thinned by the harrow and several weedings given. There are three or more pluckings when the crop is ready, and the seed cotton is carefully dried in the sun before being carted to the mills.

Manuring.

Manuring in general: Farmyard manure being used if available. Cotton is usually grown in rotation, the other crops in the rotation receiving no manure. A more or less prolonged fallow is intercalated between cotton and sessamum crops.

Tree Cottons.

"The possibility of successfully cultivating tree cottons in Burma on a commercial scale has not yet been satisfactorily established." The general unsuitability of the Lower Burma climate and soil for cotton has been indicated by failure of various Egyptian and American cottons experimented with at Prome and near Rangoon. But the long-stapled Pernambuco cotton cultivated by Miss Haswell in Amherst District was good enough to take a diploma of honour at the Franco-British Exhibition (1908). A Northern Shan States variety is promising.

Seed Distribution.

There are no seed farms yet, but it is hoped to establish some soon. The Agricultural Department distributes a little seed each year—as far as possible; but the cultivator chiefly saves his own seed, or obtains it from the mills. There has been a marked deterioration in recent years. The matter is receiving attention.

Ginneries are mostly modern mills in the hands of large firms—the Burma Cotton Company and Messrs. Jamal Brothers. For home manufacturers, especially in the hills, ginning is largely done by hand. An effort is made to select seed, but it is not too carefully carried out. Seed farms under the Department of Agriculture are the only effective means of guaranteeing good seed.

Marketing the Crop.

The crop is generally bought by millers at their mills. The cultivator carts in the produce and sells for the best price he can get at the mill. Not usually bought before maturity; though since mills have been started at Myingyan, the system of brokers who buy forward has crept in, as in the rice business.

Land Ownership.

Land is chiefly held by small landowners, who will generally adopt advice which is proved to be for their benefit.

Extent of Cultivation.

"Cotton will only be a very secondary crop over the whole of Lower Burma, and in those districts of Upper Burma where irrigation can be obtained."

Now cultivated chiefly in Meiktila, Myingyan, Sagaing, Lower Chindwin, Thayetmyo. (Burmans will grow it only when the market for it is assured.)

But also to some extent in Akyab, Northern Arakan, Sandoway, Prome, Pakokku, Minbu, Magwe, Mandalay, Shwebo, Kyaukse, and Yamethin. Possible to extend it in Minbu, Pakokku, Magwe, Shwebo, Yamethin, and Prome.

	Present area. Acres.	Further area available. Acres.	
Akyab	547	100,000	—*i.e.*, for Ya mixed cultivation.
Prome..	1,529	8,000	
Amherst	—	—	
Thayetmyo	19,833	25,000	
Pakokku	377	3,397	
Minbu	2,847	—	Not known.
Magwe..	3,712	—	
Mandalay	8	—	
Shwebo	914	—	
Sagaing	48,223	nil	
Lower Chindwin ..	12,998	25,000	
Meiktila	36,161	8,380	
Myingyan	65,511	—	

Arakan might prove suitable for tree cottons.

Prome and Thayetmyo.—There is a likelihood of increase.

In main cotton belt (comprising Meiktila, Myingyan, Lower Chindwin, and Sagaing).—Possibilities of extension and improvement are not at present very encouraging, because it is a rotation crop, and because of short sowing period (limited, as a rule, to 10 days). A good year for cotton is generally a bad year for other crops.

Reasons against possibilities of extension are :—

(1) Inferiority of staple.
(2) Precariousness of the seasons.
(3) Cost of labour and transport.
(4) Conservatism of the Burman.

"Burma may have a great future in cotton, but the variety that will give it this future has yet to be discovered."

MARKETING OF COTTON.

By far the largest proportion of the Indian crop is sent to Bombay, where it is mostly stored in the open air on the Bombay "Cotton Green." Hundreds of thousands of bales are lying in stacks neatly packed, but entirely unprotected from the weather. Men, smoking cigars and pipes, pass to and fro between the stacks, and it is almost a miracle that fires do not occur more frequently. Owing to the recent extensive destruction of cotton by fire on the "Green," it is hoped that preventive measures will be taken. The Bombay Cotton Trade Association, Limited, has its Exchange or Sale Rooms on the Cotton Green, and its rules and regulations, which will be found in the appendix, govern all cotton transactions.

The cotton from the South of the Madras Presidency is shipped viâ Madras and Tuticorin.

Owing to the small margin existing during the last season between the prices of Indian and American cotton, many of the Indian Millowners have bought this season considerable quantities of American cotton. At the end of December they had on order as much as 200,000 bales of American cotton, whilst in normal years the total annual consumption varies from 15,000 to 20,000 bales only.

The transport expenses of American cotton from Liverpool to Bombay are ·46d. per lb. A Cawnpore spinner who has also bought this season American cotton informed me that all his American cotton must be repacked and pressed in Bombay on arrival, as the Insurance Companies consider the careless and defective packing of the American bales a greater risk than the well-packed Indian cotton bales. If the American cotton were not repacked in Bombay the spinner would have to pay a higher premium of insurance for the whole of his cotton store.

The final seller of Cotton goods in a small village in India.

Summary and Conclusions.

IMPROVED STAPLE COTTONS.

It is now recognised by the Government experts and others that the cultivation in India of exotic types of long staple cotton (longer than indigenous kinds) must be confined almost entirely to the irrigated districts. Whilst long staple cottons can also be produced in a few non-irrigated tracts, it has been clearly demonstrated that, with the exception of Tinnevelly cotton in Madras and Broach cotton in Gujurat, the cultivation of long staple cotton in unirrigated parts is not economically sound; the cultivation of indigenous cottons proves more remunerative to the farmer in non-irrigated tracts, owing to the higher ginning out-turn (percentage of fibre), to the higher yield per acre, and to the less attention required. Nevertheless, the prospects of the production of long staple cottons in India are decidedly favourable in the following Provinces: Sind, Punjab, Gujurat, Southern Madras, and the Central Provinces. Spinners and all interested in the cultivation of long staple cottons in India should look upon this as a definitely settled opinion, arrived at after many years of careful investigation. The prospects of an extension of the area for these cottons lie mainly in the irrigation of hitherto dry tracts.

Staple cotton of almost equal quality to Middling American, and in some cases superior, is grown in India in the following Provinces.

Madras.

Some six years ago Mr. A. Steele, of Messrs. A. & F. Harvey, detected in a gin, mixed with the ordinary Tinnevelly, an American kind of cotton, but superior to American in quality and ginning out-turn. This cotton was traced to Cambodia, in Indo-China. It has a full inch staple, is uniform and glossy, of fine fibre, and somewhat creamy in appearance. Mr. Steele found four years ago that the ginning out-turn of this cotton was 44 per cent. against the ordinary Tinnevelly of 31 per cent. lint. This, as well as the superior quality, induced him to grow on a small piece of land the seed obtained from the lot accidentally found in the gin, and from that time Cambodia cotton has made rapid progress. Three years ago the crop was 5,000 bales, last year 30,000 bales, and this year it is expected to yield 80,000 bales of 500lbs. each. This "Cambodia" is an extraordinarily heavy yielder. One may take the average per acre as 400lbs. to 500lbs. of lint, but under special conditions as much as 2,000lbs. of seed-cotton (=660lbs. lint) are said to have been picked from one acre. If one remembers that the average yield of the Indian cotton is hardly more than 100lbs., one can easily understand that this new cotton has created a great stir amongst the people. Moreover, there is the advantage that Cambodia cotton, which is known in Liverpool by the name of "Tinnevelly American," grows well in the red soil of the Madras Presidency, which so far had not been used for cotton. Chili, tobacco, and, in some cases, rice were mostly grown in this soil. The introduction of Cambodia has not, therefore, interfered with the quantity of the ordinary well-known Tinnevelly cotton which is grown in black soil. The crop of the latter is estimated this year to be about 90,000 bales. The possibilities of the extension of Cambodia are enormous. One cotton spinner, who has a thorough knowledge of the South of India, thought that in ten years' time quite a million bales of this cotton would be produced. Whilst the picking of Indian cotton generally is carried out in the most careless fashion, it is important to note that the cotton in the South of India is generally clean and carefully picked.

In the South of India the cotton mills spin 40's with Cambodia. One spinner told me that he uses it alone for a good 30's twist, and also for mixing with a low Middling American to improve the quality.

To prevent the degeneration of Cambodia cotton-seed, I think the Government would be well advised if they were to devote one large seed farm exclusively to this kind of cotton.

Sind. Egyptian cotton had been grown for several years, but owing to the insufficient water supply in the Jamrao Canal it is considered unwise to continue the cultivation of a cotton which requires so much more water than other kinds of cotton. It has therefore been decided to substitute Egyptian cotton by American, and some 40 tons of "Triumph" seed have been ordered from the British Cotton Growing Association for distribution in this district. Black Rattler American cotton has been grown by several farmers in Sind, and Messrs. Gaddum & Co., Ltd., have valued this Sind-American cotton at 1d. to 1½d. per pound more than the ordinary Sind cotton, and expressed the opinion that it is better than American seed-cotton grown in Tinnevelly. It is anticipated that Sind will produce this year 2,000 bales of American cotton of 1in. staple and white in colour, but eventually it ought to produce about 150,000 bales. It has been proved that the yield in weight per acre in the Sind district of American cotton is exactly the same as the yield of ordinary Sind cotton.

The extension of cotton growing in Sind is largely dependent upon the construction of the *Rohri* Canal and *Sukkur* Barrage.

Punjab. This season some 600 bales of an American kind have been grown along the Chenab Canal from the seed which was acclimatised in the South of India. An Indian Millowner paid, during my visit to this district, for 400 bales of this cotton the price of fully good fair American. There is an extension of the irrigation system being carried out which will be completed by 1914, and should open up a district which ought to supply very soon 50,000 bales of the same kind of cotton.

Central Provinces. 1,500 bales of Buri cotton of ⅞in. to 1in. staple have been raised last season, the whole of which has been bought by one of the Nagpur spinning mills at about ½d. per pound above Liverpool prices of Middling American. There is the possibility of extension of long staple cotton in Chattisgar, where some 15,000 bales might be grown, either of Buri or of the above-mentioned Cambodia cotton. The advantage of Buri cotton is that it grows in water-logged districts, and is quite wilt-resisting.

Gujurat. The fine cotton produced in Nausari is entirely consumed by Ahmedabad mills. This is the finest Broach cotton. In the Surat district an improved Broach cotton of $\frac{7}{8}$in. to 1in. of white colour has been produced under the guidance of the Department of Agriculture, and this year, in spite of the unfavourable weather conditions (drought), 2,400 bales of this cotton have been produced. The Bombay Millowners have established a Buying and Ginning centre for this cotton, guaranteeing the farmer 5 per cent. above the price of ordinary local cotton. There is every probability that in consequence of this inducement the cultivation of that cotton will materially increase.

Dharwar in the south of the Bombay Presidency, is known by the Dharwar American cotton, but this has degenerated, and the Department of Agriculture is replacing it by Cambodia and the improved Broach cotton from Surat.

BUYING AND GINNING CENTRES.

The Department of Agriculture has in the past encouraged farmers to take up new kinds of cotton on very small trial scales. This, according to my opinion, must result in an inadequate price being paid to the farmer. When, for instance, a man raises 20lbs. of long staple cotton and 200lbs. of ordinary short staple cotton, he cannot expect to receive a remunerative price for the 20lbs., as nobody can use such a small quantity of cotton to advantage. The collection of small lots is expensive and causes different varieties to be mixed together. *I am convinced that the Agricultural Department should not begin distributing the new kind of seed until it is quite sure that its cultivation will be remunerative to the farmer, and until it has a sufficient quantity of seed to produce several thousand bales.* Only then will the natural demand from various sources spring up. Government officials and farmers are apt to estimate the value of their produce at too high a figure, and in comparing the price of cotton raised in India with that of American cotton in Liverpool, they ought to take into consideration that Indian cotton contains a large amount of dry leaves and impurities, and is frequently subject to the admixture of inferior kinds.

The purpose of the Buying Agency is to guarantee the farmer a fixed premium on his long staple cotton, and to keep the superior seed apart from the ordinary kind. This can be done, in my opinion, by the European spinners without the necessity of establishing their own ginneries or buying firms in India, where, contrary to the conditions in Africa, in all the cotton-growing districts well-known European cotton firms already exist, and some of these are willing to act for the European spinners as agents between them and the long staple cotton grower. As is well known, many fraudulent practices exist in the handling of cotton in India, more so perhaps than in any other country, and the cotton buying firms established there would not be so easily duped as any new concern. Moreover, the spinner would have somebody to fall back upon, if frauds did take place. Nowhere is the cotton broker or merchant more necessary than in India.

Another difficulty is that of the various native languages, and for this reason also it would not be advisable for a European Association to embark on establishing its own Buying and Ginning Agency in India. The Bombay Millowners' Association have started recently a Buying and Ginning Agency in the neighbourhood of Surat, and are having their cotton ginned by one of the existing firms, and whatever steps are undertaken by the European spinners as to the establishment of buying centres these should be in co-operation with the Indian Millowners. The cotton would have to be sold to the highest bidder, and whether it is consumed by Lancashire, India, Japan, or the Continent does not materially matter, as a corresponding amount of American cotton will be set free.

Ginneries can be hired everywhere for a whole season, thus the danger of mixing seed of various kinds can be obviated. These ginneries would have to be hired by the firm entrusted with guaranteeing the farmer the fair price.

On these lines I am in favour of assisting the growers of long staple cotton first in Sind and Gujurat (Surat), and later in the Punjab, Dharwar, and Central Provinces. Madras Presidency does not require such a stimulus, as the natural demand for its long staple cotton is coming from all parts of the world.

An Indian spinner, who has also experience of Lancashire mills, told me that very few Lancashire spinners knew how to prepare East Indian cotton properly; he said it required extra treatment in the blowing-room owing to the dirty condition in which the cotton is generally picked in India.

Fraudulent Practices.

Flagrant fraudulent practices are carried on in Berar and the Central Provinces in connection with the damping of cotton for the purpose of increasing the weight of the bales. I am pleased to say that, as a result of my bringing this matter to the attention of the Government, they are now watching this matter and are already endeavouring to stop the watering of cotton by means of a hose-pipe. The spinners will do well to carefully examine all cotton coming from India as to any excessive damp and to report such cases to the offices of the International Federation if possible, stating the district where the cotton has been grown. The use of saltpetre and seed-cotton for weighting the bales in the north of Madras Presidency should also be stopped.

The mixing of different kinds of cotton *before* ginning is another very serious matter which ought to be prevented by the Government, because it is not only that the spinner is deceived in his purchase, but that the seed of two or three different types becomes mixed and is then sold again for sowing purposes. It is this latter circumstance which is much more serious than the first. On the one hand the Government are spending large amounts of money to keep the seed pure and improve the cotton cultivation, and on the other, the Government are allowing the ginners to counteract the benefits resulting from the efforts of the Department of Agriculture.

The mixing of various cotton and of waste-cotton from the spinning mill, such as is carried on at Hubli, ought also to receive the attention of the Government, as it must necessarily create a bad reputation for the Indian cotton, and, moreover, it should be considered a criminal offence to sell a certain kind or quality of cotton which has been intentionally depreciated by the admixture of inferior kinds and dirt.

Statistical Crop Returns.

Since drawing attention in my first report to the defective methods used for obtaining the figures of the total crop of India, various resolutions have been adopted by the cotton spinners practically all over the world recommending the adoption of a system of ginners' returns, *i.e.*, a fortnightly census of the number of bales pressed.

I was informed that the Commercial Intelligence Department had taken this matter seriously in hand, and that an effort to comply with this request will probably shortly be made. The difficulty so far exists with regard to the Native States where a large amount of cotton is grown. The Governments of these cannot be forced to supply statistical information of any kind, but as some of the Native States have even recognised the usefulness of higher agricultural work and have established their own Departments of Agriculture with European experts at the head, it is evident that from the more important and enlightened Native States these returns would be forthcoming.

The spinners will do well to see that a trial of the fortnightly ginners' returns is made in India.

Department of Agriculture.

The Directors of Agriculture are members of the Indian Civil Service and occupy these positions frequently for short periods only. Their functions are mostly administrative. The technical experts are the Deputy Directors of Agriculture, whose position is inferior to the former. The Deputy Directors are men who have been trained at a British University and have had experience in practical farming. The Government must be congratulated upon the excellent selection they have made for these posts. I found the Deputy Directors all hard-working, and taking a keen interest in their duties.

The enormous tracts of country which they have to cover are such that it is impossible for them to visit all the outlying districts, and it is therefore of the utmost importance that Government should be induced to *engage at least for every Province an additional European duly qualified agricultural expert.* There would then be three European Deputy Directors in each Province, and I do not think it is too much to ask that one of these should specialise on one of the most important crops, viz., cotton. Hitherto the work of the Deputy

Directors has been too diversified; it cannot be expected that they are competent to deal satisfactorily with 15 to 20 different kinds of crops.

One mistake which is made in many of the Provinces by Deputy Directors is that they are experimenting with too many kinds of cotton. Seed is given out of about five or six different varieties, whilst it would be, in my opinion, more advantageous if the distribution of seed were confined to fewer kinds in each Province. Where different seeds are given out each type should be confined to certain villages in order that the mixing of the different types may not be easy.

I was informed that the post of Inspector-General of Agriculture will shortly be abolished. I regret this, because through this official the various Provincial Departments have communicated and exchanged their experiences. It is intended that there should be more frequent Congresses of Agricultural experts, where they can discuss and exchange experiences gained, but I believe that there should be at least one official in high authority who should permanently see to this extremely useful work. The travelling expenses in connection with these Congresses will be exceedingly heavy. The item expended on travelling expenses alone for the last of these meetings would pay the salaries of a few permanent officials.

Wherever deep-rooted weeds, such as "Heriali," exist, the Agricultural Department ought to provide *deep-working ploughs,* either driven by steam or worked by bullocks, such as described in connection with the work of the Agricultural Department in Bombay. These ploughs should be hired out at a low rate to the farmers. This is a very practical kind of work which the Department of Agriculture or some other governing body might very usefully undertake. An important extension of the cultivable area would necessarily follow.

The Government ought to realise that, India being the second largest supplier of cotton in the world, it does not spend anything like a proper proportion of the amount which the principal cotton supplying country, the United States of America, annually spends in increasing and improving its cotton crop. India spends Rs. 423,723 in the Imperial Department of Agriculture, and the eight Provincial Departments spend Rs. 2,631,218, together Rs. 3,055,000, or about £200,000. The United States Government appropriates for the Department of Agriculture $17,000,000, or about £3,500,000; in addition to this each American State makes a large appropriation from its own revenue. There can be little doubt that of the two countries more should be expected from the Government in a country where the cultivators are not yet so advanced as in the U.S.A., and where the climatic and soil conditions are much more varied.

Seed Farms.

The system adopted by the Central Provinces of having two or more "nucleus" seed farms owned by the Government and a large number of smaller seed farms owned by intelligent cultivators, spread all over the Province, is to my mind the most essential means for improving the staple and of increasing the yield. Such seed farms are especially required in the Bombay Presidency, in the Punjab, and the United

PRESS REPORTS

dealing with the Salzburg Meetings of the Committee of the International Federation of Master Cotton Spinners' and Manufacturers' Associations, and with the Secretary's Report on his visit to India.

THE COTTON INDUSTRY.

MEETING OF INTERNATIONAL COMMITTEE.

VISIT TO EGYPT.

(FROM OUR CORRESPONDENT.)

SALZBURG (AUSTRIA), Monday.

Meetings of the Committee of the International Cotton Federation were held here to-day, under the presidency of Sir Charles Macara. The countries represented were England, Switzerland, France, Germany, Austria, India, Belgium, Italy, Japan, Portugal, Spain, Norway, Sweden, and Denmark.

Herr Kuffler presented a report on the percentage of damp found by scientific investigation in cotton yarns of various counts and qualities, and was followed by Professor Reinhardt, of Reichenburg, who gave interesting details of some of the tests which have been made. The Committee decided that the investigations should be continued.

Mr. H. Kern, chairman of the Liverpool Bills of Lading Conference, urged the Committee, and through them the spinners of the world, to accept from September 1st next none but through bills of lading of which copies have been verified by the Central Bureau or by any other controlling office which the Liverpool Cotton Bills of Lading Conference Committee may at any time appoint. The Committee decided to bring this recommendation before the attention of the affiliated societies without delay, and expressed high appreciation of the admirable manner in which Mr. Kern had handled a difficult and intricate matter.

The Committee resolved that in October next an international delegation should visit Egypt and make a tour of the cotton-growing areas of that country. The Secretary reported that the Khedive, Lord Kitchener, and the Egyptian Prime Minister were taking deep interest in the proposed visit, and would personally receive the deputation and do all in their power to ensure the success of the visit. Great efforts are in progress to improve the quality of Egyptian cotton and to increase the area of land in Egypt under cotton cultivation. The visit, it is believed, will materially assist these efforts, which are of great importance to the industry, Egyptian cotton being a considerable proportion of the world's supply.

COTTON FROM INDIA.

THE NEED FOR INCREASED OUTPUT.

INTERNATIONAL COMMITTEE'S RECOMMENDATIONS.

(FROM OUR CORRESPONDENT.)

SALZBURG (AUSTRIA), Tuesday.

The International Cotton Committee concluded their sittings, under the presidency of Sir Charles Macara, and adjourned to a meeting to be held in Paris after their return from the Egyptian cotton fields.

After hearing the report of a special committee who have studied the question of cotton growing in India, the Committee recommended :

That Bills should be introduced into the Indian Legislatures making the damping of cotton a penal offence.

That tenants leasing land alongside irrigation canals should give an undertaking to devote a certain proportion of the land to cotton cultivation, under the direction of the respective Agricultural Departments.

That seed farms should be established in all cotton-growing provinces.

That the Agricultural Departments of India be recommended to obtain statistical values of crops on the lines adopted in the United States.

That everything possible be done to encourage the growth of Cambodia cotton in Southern India and cotton from American seed in Sind and Punjab.

Mr. S. M. Johnson then gave an interesting account of the cultivation of cotton in the United Provinces, and a resolution was adopted urging the Government of India to devise some scheme whereby adequate remuneration would be given to the growers of improved staple cotton. It was felt that the putting into operation of a scheme of this nature would be a great encouragement to the farmers to devote more attention to the production of longer staple cotton.

Sir Charles Macara heartily thanked Mr. Johnson for the many valuable suggestions which his long experience in India had enabled him to give the Committee, both with regard to improving the quality of the cotton and to increasing the area under cultivation ; and added that a survey of the whole of the evidence showed that the area under cotton cultivation in India could be largely increased without in any way interfering with the area devoted to growing food.

Signor Mylius (Italy) reported on the progress made with the arrangements for settling by arbitration in all European countries disputes arising out of yarn and cloth contracts. The facts convinced him, he said, that the judgments given by arbitration courts would be no more difficult to enforce than judgments given by law courts. The moral effect of the arbitration awards would be very good, and the awards themselves would be valuable documentary evidence in the event of the disputants going to law. Signor Mylius was heartily thanked, and was requested to continue his efforts.

The Committee were informed that systematic tests for damp in cotton are now being made in France and Germany on a large scale, and expressed the hope that other countries would follow the example.

Enquiries instituted by Sir Charles Macara elicited the information that the world-wide depression in the cotton trade in recent years, due to the scarcity and the high price of the raw material and the consequent reduction in the consumption of goods, was passing away, except in one or two places, and that the outlook was improving. The hope was expressed that the price of cotton would be maintained at a fair level, which would encourage growers to extend the area devoted to cotton production.

At the close of the meetings, Senor Calvet, on behalf of the Spanish cotton spinners and manufacturers, presented to Sir Charles Macara a handsome replica of the Order of the Gran Cruz del Merito Agricola, conferred on him last year by the King of Spain.

COTTON SUPPLY.

POSSIBILITIES OF INDIA AND EGYPT.

SIR CHARLES MACARA'S VIEWS.

Sir Charles Macara, who returned on Saturday from Austria, where meetings of the Committee of the International Cotton Federation were held last week, was interviewed by a press representative on his arrival.

Sir Charles said that the International Cotton Federation, which was initiated in 1904, had made a departure this year in omitting the usual Congress. It was felt last year, when the Congress was held in Spain and Portugal, that the work of the Committee had become so onerous that this experiment might be tried, especially as a discussion then took place as to whether it would not be advisable, in the interests of the cotton trade of the world, that an international delegation should visit Egypt in the coming autumn. The decision to adopt this suggestion, which was come to by the International Committee at Salzburg last week, practically meant the holding of a Congress in Egypt. Sir Charles recalled the visit of an international delegation of cotton spinners to the United States in 1907, when the information exchanged between cotton growers and cotton spinners proved of the greatest value. It was well known that the waste and extravagance of the old-fashioned methods led to a very serious enhancement in the price of the raw material. An adequate supply of the raw material at a reasonable price was essential to the prosperity of the cotton industry, but adequate remuneration for the planter must always be a primary condition.

Adoption of Modern Methods.

"If large savings are effected by the adoption of modern methods of cultivation," Sir Charles proceeded, "and prices are, as a result, reduced, the effect upon the consumption of cotton goods will be surprising, especially in the case of the 700,000,000 people in India and China. In my opinion a stable government in China would bring about such a development in the cotton industry as would provide full employment for all the machinery in the mills, notwithstanding the great increase in the number of spindles that has taken place during the past few years. Of course, it must be remembered that the cotton industry supplies by far the largest proportion of the clothing for the people of the world, and in the development I am speaking of the price of the raw material would, of necessity, play an important part. It is imperative, therefore, that the present sources of supply of the raw material should be extended, and that encouragement should be given to the cultivation of cotton wherever it can be suitably grown.

" In this connection I have been much impressed with the possibilities in our Indian Empire. The Committee was fortunate in having with them as the representative of India, on this occasion, Mr. S. M. Johnson, of Cawnpore, who has devoted many years to the study of the growing and manufacture of cotton in India. Climate, soil, a population of agriculturists, and splendid means of transport, all combine to single out India as being the country from which the present generation of cotton spinners and manufacturers may reasonably look for the speediest and much-needed increase in the supply of the raw material for their industry. India would benefit materially from such a development, which could be brought about without any interference with her food crops. Egypt has played an important part in the production of the finer growths of cotton, and it is very fitting that the international delegation now decided upon should visit that country in the autumn. The Khedive, his Prime Minister, and his advisers, are taking a deep interest in the development of the cotton crop, and Viscount Kitchener, who besides being a distinguished soldier is a great administrator and a splendid business man, is doing his utmost not only to extend the area of cultivation, but to improve the quality of the growth. Cotton cultivation is the all-important factor in the prosperity of Egypt, and its development should receive all the support and encouragement that can be given to it by cotton spinners.

Value of International Organisation.

" Each succeeding year serves to reaffirm the absolute need for the existence of an international organisation such as the International Cotton Federation. Although England owns nearly half the cotton machinery of the world, she only consumes, on account of her finer productions, about one-fifth of the world's cotton crop. It is thus only by co-operating with the other nations of the world engaged in the growing and manufacturing of cotton, that the problems confronting the industry can be satisfactorily dealt with. In the nine years that have elapsed since the initiation of the International Federation, 13 volumes of reports have been issued in three languages and circulated throughout the world. With all this information available it is to be hoped that reckless extension of machinery will cease ; this extension has taken place without regard either to the raw material available, to the supply of labour, or the consumption of the products of the cotton mills.

" The comparatively little commercial competition between the different nations engaged in producing cotton goods has been demonstrated unmistakably, and in taking the lead in this international movement England has only been performing a duty to the other nations, who, as consumers of her products, provide so large a proportion of the employment for her spindles and looms. During the past 20 years I have been obliged to study the best means of promoting harmonious relationships between capital and labour. The International Cotton Federation has demonstrated in a remarkable manner the interdependence of the nations of the world, and it has been the means of extending the good feeling which ought to prevail among the peoples of all nations. I cannot help thinking that the more statesmen of the various countries co-operate with the practical men responsible for the carrying on of the great industries, the sooner will the rivalries and jealousies between nations disappear, for we cannot lose sight of the fact that the nations of the world cannot prosper except through international trading."

Secretary's Report on his Second Visit to India.

COTTON-GROWING IN INDIA.

The complete report on the second visit to India of Mr. Arno Schmidt, the secretary of the International Cotton Federation, will be submitted to the meeting of the Committee of the Federation to be held at Salzburg on May 14th and 15th, and in the meantime an extract from it has been issued. Mr. Schmidt's business in India was mainly to investigate the possibilities of cotton growing there, "especially with a view to the study of the question of establishing cotton buying and ginning agencies in the long-staple cotton-growing districts," and his conclusion is that generally any attempt to cultivate long-staple cotton where there is no irrigation is economically unsound. Yet in certain provinces the prospects of the long staple are favourable, and the spread of irrigation should mean increasing quantities of good-class cotton. Mr. Schmidt suggests, however, that a condition of the tenancy of new land now opened out by irrigation should be the cultivation of cotton, under the direction of the Agricultural Department, on a certain proportion of it, and he mentions precedents for this preferential treatment. It is desirable, however, that the farmers should not be encouraged to raise very small crops of long-staple cotton, as the difficulty in marketing small quantities tends to make the prices very poor, and so to give them a wrong idea of what a normal industry would be. The great bulk of Indian cotton is, of course, short staple, and not very popular in the mills of Lancashire, but Mr. Schmidt quotes the opinion of an Indian spinner that very few Lancashire spinners know how to prepare it properly; he said "it required extra treatment in the blowing-room owing to the dirty condition in which the cotton is generally picked in India." Water is the obvious cure for dirt, but it is to be feared that the Indian ginneries can hardly cover a scandal with a truism.

THE COTTON AREA.

There is undoubtedly a general awakening to the desirability both of extending the range of the cotton-growing area, and of mitigating by the united action of spinners the evils which have in the past resulted from the uncertainty of supply. The International Federation has done good work in this direction, and a wise move is being made in deciding to send a delegation to Egypt in the autumn. Determined efforts are being put forward in that country to improve the quality of the crop, on which prosperity so largely depends. Lord Kitchener is displaying the zeal and energy which have in other spheres overcome all obstacles, and he promises to supplement the military fame won in the lands watered by the Nile by most successful civil administration. The proposed visit of experts will necessarily be of considerable assistance, so that the future before the Egyptian cotton growers is distinctly bright. In India also the outlook is good. The report compiled by the secretary of the Federation for this week's meeting of the International Committee states that there is not the least doubt that the crop there can be doubled without interfering with the growing of food supplies. Owing to the prolonged drought in the western districts the output during the present year will be smaller than last, but in spite of temporary setbacks the yield per acre is gradually improving. A great factor in the advance is the extension of irrigation, the importance of which is now fully recognised by the authorities as well as by all engaged in the industry. A point to which Mr. Schmidt directs notice is the need of the appointment by the Government of an additional European, who is a duly qualified agriculturist, at least for every province, in order that each may enjoy the services of an expert specialising on cotton. It is urged that continued interest must be shown by the cotton industry in the cultivation of the raw material in India, or there will be danger of sugar growing or some other branch of activity occupying the foremost attention of the Agricultural Department. As is well known, cotton is also receiving attention in many other parts of the British Empire, and in due course we may expect to be quite independent of the American fields of supply, as ought to be the case, as speedily as possible. A further indication of the same nature is the resolve to cultivate the crop on an extensive scale in Russian Turkestan. Treaty troubles with the United States have provided a stimulus for the Russians to endeavour to grow their own cotton. Here again the main problem is the need of irrigation, but the Duma has just adopted a resolution in favour of attracting private capital to help towards its solution.

INDIAN COTTON GROWING.

POSSIBILITIES OF THE INDUSTRY.

THIS YEAR'S CROP.

The possibilities of cotton growing in India have been further investigated by Mr. Arno Schmidt, the secretary of the International Cotton Federation, who has recently paid a second visit to the country with this object in view. Mr. Schmidt's investigations have been made specially with a view to the study of the question of establishing cotton buying and ginning agencies in the long staple cotton-growing districts. Mr. Schmidt has compiled a report for the International Committee, which meets at Salzburg on the 13th and 14th of this month, and from this report we are able to give the following extracts :

Improved Staple Cottons.

The cultivation of exotic long-staple cotton in India must be confined almost entirely to the irrigated districts. The cultivation of indigenous cottons, owing to the higher ginning out-turn (percentage of fibre), to the higher yield per acre, and to the lesser attention required, proves more remunerative to the farmer in non-irrigated tracts. Nevertheless, the prospects of long-staple cottons in India are decidedly favourable in the following provinces : Sind, Punjab, Gujurat, Southern Madras, and Central Provinces. The prospects of an extension of the area for these cottons lie mainly in the irrigation of hitherto dry tracts. Suitable tracts of good cotton-growing land will shortly be opened up through irrigation, and he suggests that the new land should only be leased to tenants who would be willing to cultivate a certain proportion of it with cotton, in accordance with the directions of the Agricultural Department. A similar undertaking was given by the colonists along the Jumna Canal in Sind with regard to the cultivation of Egyptian cotton.

Cambodia Cotton.

Long-staple cotton of almost equal quality to Middling American, and in some cases superior to this, is grown in several provinces. In Madras, some six years ago, Mr. A. Steele, of Messrs. A. & F. Harvey and Co., detected in a gin, mixed with the ordinary Tinnevelly, an American kind of cotton superior in quality and ginning out-turn. The origin of this cotton has been traced to Cambodia, in Indo-China. The cotton has a full inch staple, is uniform and glossy, of fine fibre, and somewhat creamy in appearance. Mr. Steele found that the ginning out-turn of this cotton was 44 per cent. against the ordinary Tinnevelly of 31 per cent. fibre four years ago. Three years ago the crop was 5,000 bales, this year it is expected to yield 80,000 bales of 500lbs. each. This "Cambodia" is an extraordinary heavy yielder. Moreover there is the advantage that Cambodia cotton, which is known in Liverpool by the name of "Tinnevelly American," grows well in the red soil of the Madras Presidency, which so far had not been used for cotton. The introduction of Cambodia has not interfered with the quantity of the ordinary well-known Tinnevelly cotton which is grown in black soil. The crop of this latter is estimated this year to be about 90,000 bales of 500lbs. each. The possibilities of the extension of Cambodia are enormous. One cotton spinner, who has a thorough knowledge of the South of India, thought that in ten years' time quite a million bales of this cotton would be produced.

Sind.

Egyptian cotton had been grown for several years, but owing to the insufficient water supply in the Jamrao Canal it is not wise to continue the cultivation of a cotton which requires more water than other kinds of cotton. "Black Rattler" American cotton has been grown by several farmers in Sind, and Messrs. Gaddum & Co. have valued it at 1—1½d. per lb. more than the ordinary Sind cotton, and expressed the opinion that it is better than American seed cotton grown in Tinnevelly. It is anticipated that Sind will produce this year 25,000 bales of American cotton of 1in. staple and white in colour, but eventually Sind ought to produce about 150,000 bales of long-staple cotton.

PUNJAB.

This season some 600 bales of an American kind have been grown along the Chenab Canal from the seed which was acclimatised in the South of India. There is an extension of the irrigation system being carried out which will be completed by 1914, and should open up a district which ought to supply at once 50,000 bales of the same kind of cotton. In the Central Provinces 1,500 bales of Buri cotton of ⅞in. to 1in. staple were raised last season, the whole of which has been bought by one of the Nagpur spinning mills at about ½d. per lb. above Liverpool prices of Middling American. There is the possibility of extension of this cotton in Chattisgar, where some 15,000 bales might be grown, either of Buri or of the above-mentioned Cambodia cotton. The advantage of Buri cotton is that it grows in water-logged districts, and is quite wilt resisting.

GUJURAT.

The fine cotton produced in Nausari is the finest Broach cotton. In the Surat district an improved Broach cotton of ⅞in. to 1in. of white colour has been produced under the guidance of the Department of Agriculture, and this year, in spite of the drought, 2,400 bales of this cotton have been produced. There is every probability that the cultivation of that cotton will materially increase.

DIFFICULTIES OF THE INDIAN FARMER.

The Department of Agriculture has in the past encouraged farmers to take up new kinds of cotton on very small trial scales. This, in Mr. Schmidt's opinion, must result in an adequate price being paid to the farmer. The Agricultural Department should not begin distributing the new kind of seed until it is quite sure that its cultivation will be remunerative to the farmer, and until it has sufficient quantity of seed to raise several thousand bales. Only then will the natural demand from various sources spring up. Government officials and farmers are apt to estimate the value of their produce at too high a figure, and in comparing the price of cotton raised in India with that of American cotton in Liverpool, they invariably forget to take into consideration that Indian cotton contains a large amount of dry leaves and impurities, and is frequently subject to the admixture of inferior kinds. The purpose of the buying agency, which has been advocated as a solution of the above difficulty, is to guarantee the farmer a fixed premium on his long-staple cotton, and of keeping the superior seed apart from the ordinary kind. This can be done by the European spinners without the necessity of establishing their own ginneries or buying firms in India, where, in all the cotton-growing districts, well-known European cotton firms exist, and some of these are willing to act for the European spinners as agents between them and the long-staple growing planter. Another difficulty is that of the various native languages, and for this reason also it would not be advisable for a European Association to embark on establishing its own buying and ginning agency in India. The Bombay Millowners' Association have started recently a buying and ginning agency in the neighbourhood of Surat, and are having their cotton ginned by one of the existing firms, and whatever steps are undertaken by the European spinners as to the establishment of buying centres these should be in co-operation with the Indian millowners. On these lines Mr. Schmidt is in favour of assisting the growers of long-staple cotton first in Sind and Gujurat (Surat), and later in the Punjab, Dharwar, and Central Provinces. Madras Presidency does not require such a stimulus, as the natural demand for its long-staple cotton is coming from all parts of the world. An Indian spinner, who has also experience of Lancashire mills, told him that very few Lancashire spinners knew how to prepare East Indian cotton properly; he said it required extra treatment in the blowing room owing to the dirty condition in which the cotton is generally picked in India.

Possibilities of the Indian Cotton Crop.

The cotton crop of India this year will be smaller than last, which is due to prolonged drought in the western districts. Reliable statistical information as to the crop is not obtainable. There is not the least doubt that the cotton crop of India can be doubled without interfering with the growing of food supplies. This is the opinion of several experts interviewed, notably of the "Imperial Cotton Specialist of India." In his opinion the yield per acre has already increased, and is gradually improving. The extension of irrigation in several provinces, which is making rapid progress, is another means of enlarging the area under cotton, and notably of long-staple cotton. In conclusion, Mr. Schmidt says he cannot speak too highly of the excellent services rendered by the able Deputy Directors of Agriculture, who are the technical experts of the Government; but the enormous tracts of country which they have to cover are such that it is impossible for them to visit all the outlying districts, and it is therefore of the utmost importance that the Government should be induced to engage at least for every province an additional European duly qualified agricultural expert, and that one of these experts in each province should specialise on cotton. Unless the cotton industry shows a continued interest in the cultivation of the raw material in India, there are signs that other industries, such as the sugar industry, will claim the foremost attention of the Agricultural Department.

Taylor, Garnett, Evans, & Co., Ltd., Manchester, Reddish, and London.

Provinces. They are, as experience has shown, no expense to the Government, whilst they act perhaps more beneficially than the experimental farms run by the Agricultural Department. The "nucleus" seed farms would help to reduce the cost of the experimental farms.

THE POSSIBILITIES OF THE INDIAN COTTON CROP.

There is not the least doubt that the cotton crop of India can be doubled without even interfering with the growing of food supplies. This is the opinion of many experts I interviewed, notably that of the Imperial Cotton Specialist of India, who, perhaps, is the highest technical expert. In his opinion the yield per acre has already increased, and is gradually improving; this is the result of his personal observation of the cotton fields during more than 20 years.

The extension of irrigation in several Provinces which is making rapid progress is another means of enlarging the area under cotton, and notably of the long stapled cotton. Government should be asked when allotting new land along the irrigation canals in the Cotton Provinces to make a stipulation in the lease that a certain proportion of it should be planted under cotton in accordance with the recommendations of the Department of Agriculture of the respective Provinces. The seed for that land should be supplied against payment from the Government seed farm; such allotments will then be demonstration farms and act as a stimulus to all the surrounding districts. There will be no cost in connection with this except the supervising of the work, which can be entrusted to superior natives.

Such stipulation has already been made and has been willingly accepted by farmers along the Jamrao Canal in Sind as regards the cultivation of Egyptian cotton, and in the Punjab the Government are insisting upon farmers who have received new land rearing a number of horses, mules, and camels. There is such a large demand for this land that there will be no great difficulty in getting people to accept that stipulation, which, moreover, would not be a hardship but simply a means of convincing the cultivators of the advisability of cultivating cotton on the proper lines.

Along these canals Government ought to reserve plots of 200 to 400 acres for seed farms.

In view of the recent purchases of cotton land by several large cotton spinning concerns in America and Africa, I considered it my duty to enquire whether the Indian Government would welcome a purchase by Europeans of new cotton land along, say, the Montgomery canal. The reply received was that "it is premature to say whether such a grant could be given, as the scheme for colonisation on the Lower Bari Doab Canal has not yet been worked out by the local Government, but that if any definite proposal is laid before the Government of India it will receive their careful consideration."

Several Anglo-Indians informed me that the policy of the Indian Government was *not to encourage the acquisition of land by Europeans in India.*

Other industries, especially the sugar industry, are making every effort to increase the cultivation of their respective raw materials in

India, and the cotton spinner must undertake the same steps if he does not wish to see the area which is used at present under cotton encroached upon by other produce.

Reply to Lord Morley's Statement.

When the deputation of Indian and Lancashire cotton spinners waited upon Viscount Morley, then Secretary of State for India, on the 27th July, 1910, he made the following statement :—

> "If more cotton growing means that less wheat is to be grown and less of other food crops, then, of course, the price of food will rise and the difficulties of the Government, which are not inconsiderable already, will be increased."

I discussed this question with almost every educated agriculturist I met in India, and the following lines summarise the opinions expressed by these gentlemen :—

A famine is caused through failure or shortage of rains. Cotton is sown on all unirrigated land in India after the first rainfall, therefore it would be impossible to grow cotton on an extended area during a season with no rain or very little rain.

The farmer before deciding on the area he will sow with cotton first allots sufficient land for the production of his and his family's food supply. The surplus of foodstuff grown by cultivators serves to feed people in the nearest cities, and in some cases is for exportation. Even during famine years India exports foodstuffs, consequently an ample supply could be transported to famine-stricken districts if the cultivator had sufficient money. He can be put into possession of money solely by cultivating remunerative crops, of which cotton is certainly one.

The population in the cities of cotton growing districts gain their livelihood by handling cotton, and with an increased production of cotton their income, too, increases, and thus they would be better enabled to purchase their food from other Indian provinces. It must in this connection be remembered that certain large tracts in India must confine themselves owing to natural conditions to the growing of foodstuffs alone. Generally speaking, there is a need for specialisation in Indian agriculture. Cotton, being a very remunerative crop, ought to be given the first place in suitable districts. India is more than self-contained, and it is therefore merely a question of which crop pays best in a certain district.

Furthermore, a famine cannot be caused through any extension of the cotton area in suitable tracts, as it is impossible to grow year after year cotton on the same piece of land. Cotton must be grown in rotation with some other crop, and as the most suitable rotation crops for cotton are jowar (millet) and wheat the farmer must at all times have a portion of his land under these crops.

The opinion is generally held that if the cultivator has the money he need not starve, as somewhere in India more than ample food supply is grown, and good means of transport exist all over the vast continent. The only difficulty exists in the case of bulky fodder, but there the necessary crop rotation assists. It is the Government's duty to induce the farmer to grow that crop which is suitable to his district and is most remunerative. It should also see that he grows it in the most judicious manner.

Resolutions on Cotton Growing in India,

Unanimously adopted at the meeting of the Committee of the International Federation of Master Cotton Spinners' and Manufacturers' Associations, held at Salzburg, May 13/14, 1912.

DAMPING OF COTTON.

This Committee respectfully invites the attention of the Secretary of State and of the Government of India to the practice adopted in some parts of India by cotton-pressing companies of artificially damping cotton, and solicits the introduction of legislative measures which will prevent the systematic watering of cottons in cotton ginneries or pressing factories, or in any place set apart for the artificial damping of cotton.

ADDITIONAL EUROPEAN AGRICULTURAL STAFF.

This Committee expresses its high appreciation of the work undertaken by the various Agricultural Departments of India, and respectfully urges on the Secretary of State the absolute necessity of strengthening the European staff in every Province if the measures for the extension of cotton cultivation that have been introduced are to be given any prospect of success.

STATISTICAL RETURNS.

This Committee desires to call attention to the system in force in the United States of America, which provides for a statistical return of the number of bales of cotton pressed, the desirability of which was approved by the Sixth International Cotton Congress at Brussels, and which was urged upon the Secretary of State by a deputation of millowners from India and England. In the opinion of this meeting, the Secretary of State and the Government of India should be urged to institute a statistical return on similar lines in India.

IMPROVED STAPLE COTTON.

This Committee expresses its high satisfaction with the qualities of Cambodia cotton grown in the South of India and of American cotton grown in Sind and the Punjab, and urges the Government of India to direct the Agricultural Departments to give the utmost attention to the cultivation of these kinds of cotton and introduce measures by which in the early stages of cultivation the Agricultural Departments will be enabled to grant remunerative prices to cultivators for their out-turns of improved staples up to the time marketable quantities can be produced.

NEW COTTON LAND.

In the opinion of this Committee new land in any cotton-growing Province, along irrigation canals that are being completed, should only be leased to tenants with the stipulation that a certain portion of each holding should be cultivated with cotton under the direction of their respective Agricultural Departments.

SEED FARMS.

This meeting respectfully requests the Government of India to establish a system of seed farms in all the cotton-growing Provinces of India on the lines of those instituted by the Central Provinces' Department of Agriculture, which have been an unqualified success, as it is of opinion that only by such a system of seed farms, distributed all over the provinces, can suitable strains of cotton be kept pure. That such seed farms are, in addition, most valuable for purposes of practical demonstration, and are capable of being worked, if properly managed, free of cost to the Government.

MIXING OF COTTON.

This Committee respectfully draws the attention of the Government of India to the fraudulent practices of mixing waste with cotton, and also of mixing inferior grades of cotton with staple grades in some cotton ginneries. They are advised this adulteration takes place quite openly, and that the waste and inferior cotton are frequently brought long distances by railway. The Committee suggests that possibly steps could be taken by Executive Officers to check these practices.

APPENDIX.

Note on the Work of the Agricultural Department in the United Provinces (India) in connection with the Cultivation of Cotton.

Written for the Upper Indian Chamber of Commerce by Mr. S. M. JOHNSON, Cawnpore, and presented to the Committee of the International Federation of Master Cotton Spinners' and Manufacturers' Associations, at the meeting in Salzburg, May 14th, 1912.

The gross area of the United Provinces and Oudh as shown in statistical tables published by Government is about $61\frac{1}{5}$ million acres. Of this area there are on an average $2\frac{4}{5}$ million acres under forests; $9\frac{3}{5}$ million acres are occupied by townships, villages, canals, railways, &c., and $35\frac{2}{5}$ million acres are cultivated, leaving $10\frac{1}{5}$ million acres of culturable waste and $3\frac{1}{5}$ million acres of current fallows.

(2) Of the $35\frac{2}{5}$ million acres of cultivated land, about $5\frac{3}{5}$ millions are cropped twice, giving a total of about 41 million acres. Of this area 36 million acres are under food crops and 5 million acres under non-food crops; and of the latter $1\frac{2}{5}$ million acres are on an average under cotton.

(3) Of the 36 million acres under food crops nearly 9 million are irrigated, and of the $1\frac{2}{5}$ million acres under cotton about one-third are irrigated.

(4) Of the land under cotton nearly the whole area is comprised within the four divisions of Meerut, Agra, Rohilkhund, and Allahabad in the Provinces of Agra; the land under cotton in the Province of Oudh (which consists of the Lucknow and Fyzabad Divisions), being only 50,000 acres.

(5) The above figures show generally that the Eastern Districts of the United Provinces are unsuited to the growth of cotton: there being 9 million acres under other crops than cotton in the Province of Oudh with only 50,000 acres under cotton, while in the Province of Agra 25 million acres are under other crops and $1\frac{2}{5}$ millions under cotton.

ESTABLISHMENT.

The Department that has the supervision of these 61 million acres is the Department of Land Records and Agriculture. It is divided into two branches, viz.:—

1. Land Records;
2. Agriculture;

with one supreme head controlling both branches, viz., The Director of Land Records and Agriculture.

(2) The Director has under him one Dy. Director for the Land Records Branch, but as this branch, with its large staff of Putwaris and Kanungos, has nothing to do with the present investigation, no further reference will be made to it.

(3) The Second Branch, viz., Agriculture, is under the same supreme head as the Land Records Branch, but is sub-divided into three sections, as follows :—

1. Agricultural College;
2. Research;
3. Practical Agriculture;

each being immediately subordinate to the supreme head, the Director.

(4) The staff of the control of these sections is as follows :—

College. A Principal.

Research. A Botanist and Assistant Botanist, and a Chemist.

Practical. Two Deputy Directors and one Assistant Director.

(5) With the College these notes have no concern. In the Research Branch, the Botanist, Mr. Martin Leake, is almost entirely engaged in researches into the growth of the cotton plant; sorting out and growing pure strains; crossing pure strains, and generally endeavouring to obtain a plant suited to the conditions of cultivation in the United Provinces and possessing a lint of superior quality and heavy production. The results of his work will be referred to later on in these notes.

(6) For administrative purposes the practical branch of the Agricultural Department is divided into three circles, each directly under the supreme head, viz., the Director. The three circles are :—

The Western Circle.
The Central Circle.
The Eastern Circle.

(7) The two former are each under a Deputy Director, and the latter under an Assistant Director. The Western and Central Circles being practically the only cotton growing circles there will be no further reference to the Eastern Circle.

(8) In the Western Circle Dr. Parr is the Deputy Director in charge, and in the Central Circle Mr. Burt. These two officers have entire charge of all Agricultural operations and experiments in their respective circles under the immediate orders of the Director.

(9) I have so far indicated the land areas in the United Provinces and the areas under food crops, non-food crops, and cotton respectively, and will now treat of the practical part of my investigation.

COTTON SEED FARMS.

There are no cotton seed farms anywhere in the United Provinces. By seed farm is meant land set apart by Government and maintained by it for the cultivation of any desired quality of cotton, and the ultimate distribution of the seed so obtained among cultivators. I am informed that Government has recently acquired 200 acres of land as an experimental farm at Allygur which will be under the charge of Mr. Martin Leake, for the cultivation of the particular cotton he has been experimenting upon. This grant is one for which all interested in cotton should be thankful, as being at last a step in the right direction, and if the particular cotton that is now to be experimented with there is not a success the land and organisation will be ready for the reception of other varieties. It must be remembered that the success or failure of any particular variety takes at least one year to ascertain, and that progress must necessarily be slow. A cotton cannot be recommended to the cultivator by the Agricultural Department until it has been proved to be a success by that department, for failure would be disastrous.

EXPERIMENTAL FARMS.

There is land set apart by Government in Cawnpore (about 80 acres) and in Allygur (about 90 acres) which has been for many years used as Experimental Farms for cotton as well as other products, such as wheat, sugarcane, ground nuts, maize, juar, gram, &c.

(2) The Cawnpore experiments have been conducted with varieties of Desi cotton and with American cotton. The last description was experimented with for many years, but apparently never got to the stage of being passed as fit for propagation of seed for wholesale cultivation, and was finally abandoned three or four years ago. Since then experiments have been, and are being conducted with other varieties of cotton.

(3) The indigenous cottons of the United Provinces consist of many types, but they are all said to be of a single species. The simplest classification for the purpose of my notes is, I think, that which divides them into :—

White Flowers;
Yellow Flowers;
Red Flowers.

(4) White and yellow flowered cottons are found quite commonly in the fields, though yellow largely predominates, and it is from these that the Desi cotton of commerce is obtained in these Provinces. The red flower plant is an isolated type and is only found in the vicinity of temples; it has the longest staple of any of the indigenous cottons, but it is a late flowering plant, and the reason for its not being grown as a field crop is because this habit makes it a non-remunerative crop to the cultivator.

(5) Since the abandonment of the American cotton Mr. Leake has been engaged, as already stated, in cultivating pure strains of the white and yellow flowered cottons, and establishing crosses between them and the red flower and other types from other parts of India. The most successful have been with—

(*a*) white flower and red;
(*b*) yellow flower and red.

The cross (*a*) has a lint which is somewhat coarse though long, while (*b*) is silky. Neither of these crosses has yet stood the test of field conditions, but the 200 acres which Government has acquired at

Allygur, and which I have already referred to, have been placed at Mr. Leake's disposal specially for trial under field conditions of the crosses (*a*) and (*b*).

(6) At Allygur experiments on very similar lines have been carried on: in that direction distribution of American seed was made on fairly large scale, but the attempt to establish it ended in failure, and I understand the cultivators in this district will have nothing to do with acclimatised American seed, so that in this district also experiments with American seed have been a failure and have been abandoned.

(7) Experiments in Allygur as in Cawnpore have also been carried on with other descriptions of cotton, and the Deputy Director there, Dr. Parr, in the course of his experiments found in two villages the white flowered types of cotton (ante) which the cultivators in these two villages had preserved as a pure strain because it was a more abundant producer than the common Desi in other villages.

(8) Dr. Parr accordingly took up this particular cotton and experimented with it: these experiments have been carried on for three years, the method followed being to distribute seed from the farm and elsewhere to picked cultivators in the surrounding villages, offering to compensate in the event of failure, watching progress, and buying back the seed resulting from the ensuing growth.

(9) The results of these experiments are that in the season just ended Dr. Parr has been able to collect about 250 maunds of seed; this seed will now be sold to cultivators (who now clamour for it), and the next growing season (June to September, 1912) it is hoped there will be fully 3,000 acres in Allygur District under White Flower. Dr. Parr proposes collecting as much of this seed as possible again next year, so as to preserve the pure strain, and again distributing it; he hopes there will be at least 30,000 acres under White Flower in the Season 1913.

DEMONSTRATION FARMS.

(1) There are no Demonstration Farms especially so-called in these Provinces.

(2) Mr. Schmidt, the Secretary of the International Spinners' Federation, appeared to attach importance to them, but Experimental Farms might also be called Demonstration Farms, since they are available in common with any other Farms for demonstration purposes. Besides, any field in the vicinity of a village could be made use of for demonstration purposes, so that there appears to be no need at all to set aside special lands as Demonstration Farms.

GENERAL.

(1) It will be seen from the foregoing that the only lands available for experiments in cotton growing are the areas at Cawnpore and Allygur; that these lands comprise many other products and are not by any means confined to cotton; and that there are no seed farms at all.

(2) The cause of this state of affairs was no doubt due to the fact that when the experiments with American cotton were finally abandoned the Department had nothing to fall back upon: it then became necessary to discover some cotton which might eventually be found to be better than the ordinary Desi plant found in the fields.

(3) Long before American cotton was abandoned as a failure in these Provinces the opinion of experts and of the Upper India Chamber of Commerce was that the only hope of success lay in improving indigenous cottons, and this advice pressed upon the Government in season and out of season has at last come to be found sound and correct and is now followed.

(4) The cottons Mr. Leake and Dr. Parr are now engaged upon are purely indigenous types; the crosses Mr. Leake has cultivated and Dr. Parr's White Flower promise a cotton far superior to the present Desi in all desirable characteristics, the main ones being that it picks clean and produces a ginning percentage of nearly 40 against about 33 of the ordinary Desi, and that it has a longer staple.

METHODS SUGGESTED FOR THE IMPROVEMENT OF COTTON CULTIVATION IN THE UNITED PROVINCES.

(1) It has been shown that there are only 80 acres in Cawnpore and 90 acres in Allygur used as Farms in these Provinces for every variety of product, and further land to the extent of 200 acres at Allygur is to be acquired.

(2) But this is not enough; Government should have a properly equipped Farm in each of the great cotton growing districts; and as a season lost means at least a delay of one year, endeavours should be made to have these farms equipped and ready before the rainy season of 1913.

(3) I understand land for a Farm of about 100 acres could be acquired and equipped with all the necessary appurtenances, cattle, huts, houses, &c., for under 40,000 Rs. Only about 30 acres of this would be available for cotton, as the latter could only be sown in rotation with other crops.

(4) These farms would always be self-supporting, and would always yield Government a fair return on the capital spent. Moreover, practically the whole of the capital would always be realisable as, if or when relinquished, the land could always be sold again.

(5) It appears to me there ought to be at least five additional Farms acquired and equipped this year. One has already been sanctioned at Allygur; there should be another at Cawnpore, one at Meerut, one at Agra, and one at or near Kulpahar, in Bundelkhand.

(6) The Farms at Cawnpore and Kulpahar would be Experimental Farms at first; the former to experiment with the White Flowered cotton and the latter to experiment with Kulpahar cotton, which is a superior cotton to the ordinary Desi and fetches a higher price.

(7) Agra and Meerut would be seed Farms to propagate the seed of the White Flower already established in the District, while the additional farm at Allygur would be for Mr. Leake's crosses. Should Mr. Leake's cotton be found to be satisfactory under the tests that are about to be applied then these would supplant the White Flower as being a superior cotton.

(8) In his reply to the Deputation that waited on him in 1910, Lord Morley said that Government could not be expected to do anything which would diminish the area under food crops, but the risk in non-food crops, and particularly cotton, ever encroaching on the food crops of these provinces appears to be absolutely non-existent;

60 per cent. of the land in the United Provinces is under food crops, while only about 2·3 per cent. is under cotton.

(9) I hear the Government contemplate reviving the cultivation of American cotton. I think we must all hope that there is no truth in the rumour. The history of the numerous and long-continued experiments with this cotton is too recent to be forgotten and is nothing but a record of many years lost : much money spent on which there has been no return, and failure and abandonment everywhere.

(10) Endeavouring to grow American cotton in the United Provinces appears to me much as if one tried to breed race horses in them—the necessity of continuously importing the pure strain in order to keep up the type would be so expensive as to put it entirely out of the reach of the cultivator, apart altogether from all other considerations.

(11) Thirty years ago the Agricultural Department in these Provinces tried experiments here in Cawnpore between New Orleans and Upland (both American) on the one hand, against Kulpahar (Bundelkhand) and common Desi on the other hand. The results went to show that the indigenous cotton was by far the most profitable. These were the results as reported by the Department itself, and in its own words.

(12) As regards improved methods of cultivation it appears difficult to say anything in a country where, for instance, the best and latest ideas in ploughs which will turn over the soil to a depth of 8 or 9 inches are scornfully rejected in favour of one which merely scratches the surface. A great deal appears to depend on the cultivator himself; one individual will thin out weak-looking plants and thus secure only vigorous growths, while another will allow all to grow up together; one will try and secure a pure strain (as in the villages in the Allygur District already referred to), while another leaves everything to fate.

STAFF.

Any extra Farms that may be established must, I should think, be placed under the control of competent natives, of whom there are many, no doubt, available, but their supervision by a European Officer with Western training would be essential, and I doubt if the existing staff of Two Deputy Directors could carry on the extra duties.

(2) The value of European Officers coming into frequent contact with cultivators in surrounding villages : of personally knowing them, taking an interest in their fields and inculcating Western ideas, whether the former follow them or not, must be so enormous that any question of cost ought to be of no consideration. I was much impressed with the work done by Dr. Parr in Allygur. He is in close touch with all the villages that grow White Flowered cotton : he sells the seed to them and arranges for their Kuppas to be ginned and after selling the cotton he buys back the seed : this seed he again sells to selected cultivators and thus keeps the strain pure.

(3) It is only by measures such as these that he is able to look forward to having 30,000 acres under White Flower in the season 1913.

BOMBAY COTTON TRADE ASSOCIATION, LIMITED.
BY-LAWS.

(1) The official year of the Association shall be from 1st November to 31st October, and the annual subscription shall be as follows, and must be paid to the Secretary not later than November 15th in each year.

(2) No persons shall be admitted to the premises of the Association unless they are shareholders or ticketholders under one of the following rules:—

(*a*) *Members* shall consist of firms or companies whose representative is, or representatives are, shareholders in the Bombay Cotton Trade Association, Limited. Members shall pay a subscription of Rs. 100 per annum. This shall entitle them to have surveys held on their cotton and to receive six entrance tickets for their nominated employés, who shall be allowed to use the rooms, provided their names have been previously submitted to the Secretary and endorsed on the tickets.

(*b*) *Associate Members.*—Firms or persons, who wish to become Associate Members, and so have the use of the rooms, and the right of having surveys held on their cotton, must send in an application (on a form to be obtained from the Secretary) to the Board of Directors, and provided their application is approved of by three of the Directors and the applicants pay a subscription of Rs. 50 per annum, they shall be considered duly elected as Associate Members for the official year, and shall be entitled to receive three entrance tickets for their nominated employés, who shall be allowed to use the rooms, provided their names have been previously submitted to the Secretary and endorsed on the tickets.

(*c*) *Ticket-holders, i.e.,* persons who wish to become ticket-holders, and merely to have the use of the rooms (but not the right to have surveys held on their cotton), must send in an application (on a form to be obtained from the Secretary) to the Board of Directors, and provided their applications are approved of by three of the Directors and the applicants pay a subscription of Rs. 10 per annum, they shall be considered duly elected as ticket-holders for the official year and be entitled to receive one entrance ticket each to the rooms.

N.B.—All holders of tickets shall produce the same whenever required by officers of the Association.

(3) Members may introduce strangers visiting Bombay to the premises of the Association.

RULES AND REGULATIONS FOR DELIVERIES, ARBITRATIONS, AND SETTLEMENTS OF DISPUTES.

(1) *Appeal Committee.*—The Appeal Committee (three to form a quorum) shall consist of the Board of Directors of the Association for the time being and three other Shareholders of the Association elected from time to time by the Board, but should the Members of the Appeal Committee present at any appeal consider it desirable to call in one or more Shareholders of the Association to assist them in deciding the appeal, they are hereby empowered to do so, and the Shareholder or Shareholders so appointed shall be Members of the Appeal Committee for that day only, and the award given either unanimously or by a majority of the Appeal Committee so constituted as aforesaid shall be the award of the Appeal Committee.

(2) *Quotation Committee.*—The Board shall, from time to time, appoint Daily Quotation Committees, consisting of three of the members of the Appeal Committee, for the purpose of registering the market rates of the different growths of cotton. Two to form a quorum.

(3) *Monthly Quotations.*—The Directors shall meet on or about the 25th of each month for the purpose of fixing and registering the market rates of cotton for the purpose of contracts falling due on the 25th of the month.

(4) *Daily Quotations.*—The rates so registered as aforesaid, either by the Board or the Daily Quotation Committees (in the latter case subject to the right of appeal to the Board of Directors on payment of the usual appeal fee of Rs. 50), shall be binding on all parties entering into contracts for sale or purchase of cotton according to the Rules of this Association in settling disputes with reference to the market rate of the day.

(5) *Time for Arbitrations.*—All arbitrations and appeals with reference to quality must be held in the rooms of the Association, and must be commenced not later than 5-30 p.m. (Standard Time), unless otherwise mutually agreed to. If, however, the lots of cotton tendered for arbitration on any one day are so numerous as to render it impossible for arbitrations to be commenced by 5-30 p.m. (Standard Time) on all the tenders from which samples have been drawn, either party interested shall have the right to postpone such arbitrations (on the same samples) till 5 p.m. (Standard Time) the following day. Such extension of time shall be regarded as an extension of the three days mentioned in Rule 18.

(6) *Arbitration Fees.*—The fees of arbitrators appointed under Rule 12 shall be Rs. 10 each for the first 110 bales or less, and Rs. 5 each for every additional 110 bales or less, each party to pay their own arbitrator; and in case of an umpire being called in, his fee shall be the same as the original arbitration fee and be borne by the arbitrators in equal shares.

(7) The fees of arbitrators appointed under Rule 13 shall be not less than Rs. 25 each, and be paid by the party or parties for whom they act at the time of application for arbitration. In case of an

umpire being called in, his fee shall be the same as the original arbitration fee and be borne by the arbitrators in equal shares.

(8) *Appeal Fees.*—The charge for an appeal to the Board and/or the Appeal Committee shall be Rs. 50 (except as provided for in Rule 13) and must be paid to the Association at the time an application for an appeal is made.

(9) In cases where arbitrations are held on samples sent from Japan, and either party shall be dissatisfied with the award, a right of appeal shall lie to the Appeal Committee, provided it be claimed within 7 days after the day on which the arbitration was held, and provided also that the appellant pays the appeal fee on the following scale :—

Not exceeding 300 bales					Fee Rs.	50
Above 300 bales but not exceeding 500 bales					,,	75
,, 500	,,	,,	,,	750 ,,	,,	100
,, 750	,,	,,	,,	1,000 ,,	,,	125
,, 1,000	,,	,,	,,	1,500 ,,	,,	150
,, 1,500	,,	,,	,,	2,000 ,,	,,	175
2,000 or more					,,	200

And an award signed by at least three members of the Appeal Committee and countersigned by the Secretary shall be deemed to be the award of the Appeal Committee and shall in all cases be final. The arbitration samples shall be used for the purposes of the appeal unless otherwise mutually agreed upon by both parties.

If, however, both parties to the contract should agree to the appeal being held after expiry of the seven days named above, it shall be permissible to hold it at some future time, provided fresh samples are submitted to the Appeal Committee.

(10) The Association shall collect all arbitration fees and pay the same to the arbitrators and umpires, less 10 per cent., which must be deducted and credited to the Association for general expenses. The Association shall, however, only be responsible for the fees which have actually been collected by their clerk.

(*a*) In case of appeals (regarding Rates) under Rules 4 and 14, Rs. 20 of the fee shall be credited to the funds of the Association and the balance paid in equal shares to the Directors present at such appeals.

(*b*) In case of appeals (regarding Quality) under Rules 12 and 18, Rs. 20 shall be credited to the funds of the Association and the balance paid in equal shares to the Members of the Appeal Committee who sign the award.

(*c*) In case of appeals (other than quality) under Rule 13, the whole of the fee shall be credited to the funds of the Association.

(11) No member of the Association having any interest in a matter in dispute shall vote on the question of the appointment of arbitrators or umpires, and no such members shall be competent to sit on any arbitration or appeal.

(12) *Arbitrations regarding Quality.* — All questions or disputes as to quality between buyer and seller shall be referred to the arbitration of two disinterested persons, being shareholders of the Company, one to be chosen by each disputant, such arbitrators having the power to call in a third arbitrator, who must also be a shareholder. The award made by such arbitrators or any two of them shall be final and binding, subject only to the right of appeal to the Appeal Committee.

(13) *Arbitrations other than Quality.*—All questions in dispute between buyer and seller (other than that of quality) shall be referred to the arbitration of two disinterested persons being shareholders of the Association, one to be chosen by each disputant, such arbitrators having the power to call in a third arbitrator who must also be a shareholder. The award made by such arbitrators or any two of them shall be final and binding on both parties, subject only to the right of appeal to the Board on payment of Rs. 100. Should one of the disputing parties appoint an arbitrator, and the other refuse or neglect to do so for twenty-four hours after notice in writing of the appointment, or in case the arbitrators appointed shall not, within seven days after their appointment, agree to an award or appoint a third arbitrator, or after the appointment of such third arbitrator, in case of the death, refusal to act, or incapacity of any of such three arbitrators, or in event of two out of three arbitrators not agreeing, then upon application of either of the disputing parties, the question in dispute shall stand, referred to two arbitrators, to be nominated by the Chairman of the Company for the time being, or in case of his absence, illness, or interest in the matter in dispute, then by the Deputy Chairman, if not interested, and in case of the absence of the Chairman and Deputy Chairman, their illness or interest in the matter in dispute, then by the Board, and in case the two arbitrators so appointed, whether by the Chairman, the Deputy Chairman or the Board, shall not, within seven days after their appointment, agree to an award or choose a third arbitrator, then the Board shall appoint a third arbitrator and shall, in the case of the death, refusal to act, or incapacity of any of such three arbitrators, from time to time substitute a new arbitrator in the place of the arbitrator or arbitrators so dying, refusing or being incapacitated. The arbitrators in all cases shall be shareholders of the Company. The award of any two arbitrators appointed under this rule shall be final and binding on both parties, subject only to the right of appeal to the Board on payment of Rs. 100.

(14) *Insolvency.*—If before the maturity of any contract either party shall become insolvent or bankrupt, such party shall be deemed to be unable to fulfil the contract and the other party shall forthwith buy or sell, as the case may be, in the market at a reasonable rate on the account of the insolvent or bankrupt party, and shall be entitled to receive from or shall pay to him, as the case may be, the difference (if any) between the re-purchase or re-sale price and the rate named in the contract. Provided always that if there is any dispute as to the reasonableness or otherwise of the price paid by the solvent party, when buying or selling in the market on account of the insolvent or bankrupt party, such dispute shall be referred to arbitration under Rule 13.

(15) *Delivery Order Form.*—All Delivery Orders must be in conformity with the form as printed on p. 107, which shall be known as the "Bombay Cotton Trade Association Ld.'s Official Delivery Order Form," and any Delivery Order which is not issued on such form shall not be deemed to be a valid Delivery Order within the meaning of, or acceptable under, these Rules.

(16) In every contract made under these Rules the purchaser shall be deemed (subject to the provisions of Rule 22) to have agreed to accept in fulfilment of such contract any cotton which may be passed, either without an allowance, or, with an allowance awarded on arbitration or appeal under Rule 12.

(17) All cotton contracted for, for forward delivery, shall be ready and Delivery Order for the same (as provided in Rule 15) shall be tendered by 1 p.m. (Standard Time), on the latest date for delivery specified in the contract. In case a Delivery Order for the cotton or any portion of it is not so tendered, or in case the cotton or any portion of it for which a Delivery Order has been passed is not actually then ready in Colaba on the Jaitha or in the godown for delivery, the buyer may (1) cancel the contract, or (2) buy in the market on the same day at a reasonable rate on account, and at the risk and expense of the seller, or (3) claim damages at the market rate of the day, *vide* (Rule 29); provided always that in the event of the buyer exercising the option of buying in the market, and there being any dispute as to the reasonableness or otherwise of the price paid by him, such dispute shall be referred to arbitration as provided by Rule 13. If on the other hand the seller has tendered the cotton within the time specified in the contract, as provided for above, and if the buyer neglects or refuses to either approve of, or have arbitration held on the cotton so tendered, as provided in Rule 18 hereafter, the seller, after giving 48 hours' notice to weigh after the expiration of the time allowed for arbitration, has the option of either selling the goods at the risk and expense of the buyer, or claiming damages at the market rate of the day.

(*a*) In contracts where it is not stated whether the cotton is to be Machine-ginned or Hand-ginned description, the seller shall have the right of tendering either Machine-ginned or Hand-ginned cotton or an admixture of both, provided always that the lot tendered be of one description.

(*b*) Against contracts on Rail Delivery Terms, if a Delivery Order is tendered, the sampling for arbitration or approval and weighment of such cotton shall be done in the seller's Jaitha or godown, and the buyer shall cart it from there at his own expense. In such cases no muccadum allowance shall be payable by the seller, unless it is so specified in the contract.

(*c*) Against contracts for Khamgaon and, or Akola, only cotton pressed at either of these places constitutes a fair tender, provided it is of the description sold.

(*d*) Against contracts for "Oomra, Fair Staple," only cotton pressed at the following places constitutes a fair tender, provided it is of the description sold :—

Akola.
Akote.
Balapore.
Banosa.
Boregaon.
Jalgaon-Jamod.
Karanja.
Khamgaon.
Murtizapur.
Nandura.
Paras.
Shegaon.
Telhara.

(*e*) Against contracts for Bengals, only cotton pressed at the following places constitutes a fair tender, provided it is of the description sold :—

Atrauli Road.
Aligarh.
Auriya.
Agra.
Ait.
Baran.
Barant.
Bhind.
Belanganj.
Ballabgarh.
Babrala.
Chandausi.
Cawnpore.
Dhampur.
Dibai.
Dholpur.
Damoh.
Delhi.
Delhi (Lahori Gate).
Etawah.
Firozabad.
Fatehgarh.
General Ganj (Cawnpore).
Guna.
Ganj Dundwara.
Harduaganj.
Hodal.
Hathras City.
Harpalpur.
Hapur.
Hapurganj.
Hindaun Road (Mandawar).
Houra.
Hamirpur Road.
Hurdoi.
Jhansi.
Jalesar Road.
Kerowlee.
Kanth.
Kasganj.
Kashipur.
Khorai.
Khurja.
Kanauj.
Karnal.
Karwi.
Kalpi.
Kaimganj.
Kamalganj.
Karachi (Bengal descriptions from).
Kunch.
Kulpahar.
Kosi.
Meerut Mandi.
Muttra Junction.
Mainpuri.
Mandal.
Muzaffarnagar.
Moradabad.
Meerut City.
Morena.
Nagina.
Najibabad.
Panipat.
Punjabi Serai.
Palwal.
Pathuria.
Raja Ganj.
Sikandra Rao.
Sikandrabad.
Serai Rohilla.
Sasni.
Saharanpur.
Sonepat.
Shikohabad.
Umballa City (Ambala).
Ujhani.
Ulwar (Alwar).

And all Rajputana descriptions, as defined in Rule 17 (*g*).

(*f*) Against contracts for Sind Punjab descriptions, only cotton pressed at the following places constitutes a fair tender, provided it is of the description sold:—

Amritsar.
Abohar.
Bhiwani.
Changa-Manga.
Dera Ghazikhan.
Dera Ismailkhan.
Chiniot Road.
Chunian.
Dipalpur.
Fazilka.
Ferozepore Cantonment.
Ferozepore City.
Gaujranwala.
Gobindgarh.
Gojra.
Ghotki.
Ghorabari.
Gidu Bandar.
Gote-saheb.
Hansi.
Hissar.
Hydrabad (Sind).
Jullunder.
Jhelum.
Jhind.
Karachi.
Karachi (Sind and Punjab descriptions *via* Karachi).
Kasur.
Kaithal.
Khanna.
Kot Kapura.
Kot Radhakisen.
Kotri.
Lahore.
Ludhiana.
Lyallpur.
Larkhana.
Mooltan.
Montgomery.
Malerkotla.
Mirpurkhas.
Narwana.
Narnaul.
Nabha.
Nowshera.
Okara.
Pathankot.
Peshawar.
Pattoki.
Rohtak.
Raewind.
Rawalpindi.
Rewari.
Rashida.
Ratodero.
Rohri.
Sirsa.
Sialkote.
Sirhind.
Sangla Hill.
Shadipally.
Sehwan.
Shahdadpur.
Shahbandar.
Shikarpur.
Sukkur.
Toha Tek Singh.
Tando Adam.
Tando Allahyar.
Tando Aga Ismail.
Tando Kaiser.
Tando Mohomedkhan.
Tando Jam.
Ushana.
Umarkot.
Wazirabad.
Zaferwal.

(*g*) Against contracts for Rajputana descriptions, only cotton pressed at the following places constitutes a fair tender, provided it is of the description sold:—

Barl.
Beawar.
Bhilwara.
Bundi.
Balotra.
Erinpura Road.
Kesarpura.
Kapasin.
Lambia.
Merta Road.
Nimbahera.
Nasirabad.

Falna. Rani.
Jeypore. Sanwar.
Kishengarh. Tonk.
Kotah. Tilaunia.
Kekri.

(18) The seller when issuing a Delivery Order must insert in it the price at which he requires payment and the day on which the right to hold an arbitration on the cotton will expire; no Delivery Order shall be issued unless at the time of the issue of such order the cotton is actually ready in Colaba either on the Bunder or Jaitha, or in the godown; if there should be a greater number of bales on the Bunder or Jaitha or in the godown of the mark tendered than the number specified in the Delivery Order, the buyer shall have the right to demand that the bales tendered to him be indicated specially by a distinguishing mark before sampling, but the buyer shall not have the right to object to the tender for the sole reason that the bales tendered have not been separated from other bales of the same mark.

To constitute a valid tender under these Rules the bales tendered must all be in one Jaitha or godown.

A Delivery Order can be passed on against a contract, but no person is bound to accept a Delivery Order before 10-30 a.m. (Standard Time), or after 3 p.m. (Standard Time), or after 1 p.m. (Standard Time) on the day on which the right to hold an arbitration expires, or after 1 p.m. (Standard Time) on the latest date for delivery specified in the contract.

The arbitration (if any) must be held not later than three days, after the date of the Delivery Order, and if it is not held within that time, the cotton must be taken by the buyer without arbitration.

In the event of the seller refusing or neglecting to have the arbitration held before the expiration of the three days as provided for above, the buyer shall have the right to have an *ex-parte* arbitration held, and the award in such arbitration shall be binding upon both parties subject to the usual right of appeal.

N.B.—Notice in writing, calling for an arbitration, is not necessary.

(19) For purposes of inspection, the buyer shall have the option of opening 5 per cent. of bales at the buyer's expense, in case the cotton passes without arbitration being called for, or if passed by the arbitrators.

(20) For the purposes of arbitration 10 per cent. of bales may be opened (3 per cent. of which may be opened outright), and such bales shall be re-pressed at the cost of the losing party (say, at Rs. 2 per bale). The samples are to be drawn conjointly by parties representing buyers and sellers from both sides of the bales, the buyers selecting the bales to be opened; and all samples drawn shall be used for determining the questions of either "false packing" or "quality," but due allowance shall be made for the change in the appearance of the hard side of the bale owing to cross packing.

(21) Should part only of a lot be tendered and such part be

arbitrated upon, such arbitration shall refer only to the part, and the balance of the lot shall be considered as a separate lot for arbitration. If the contract be for only 110 bales or less, only one tender shall be made; if for more and in multiples of 100 bales, the tender shall be made in multiples of 100 bales, and if the contract be in multiples of 110 bales the tender also shall be made in multiples of 110 bales.

(22) If the final award for inferiority of quality be in excess of Rs. 5 per candy (unless as provided for in exception (*a*) to this rule), or if the lot tendered be found to be a full grade below the quality contracted for, or to be fraudulently packed or damaged, the buyer shall have the option either to take the cotton at the allowance fixed by the arbitrators or the Appeal Committee, or upon giving notice in writing to the seller and original tenderer to refuse the same, in which latter case he may either buy in the market at a reasonable rate on account, risk and expense of the seller, or invoice it back to the seller at the market rate of the day upon which the final award shall have been made, provided always that in the event of the buyer exercising the option of buying in the market, he shall do so not later than the day following that on which the arbitration and/or appeal (if any) is finally disposed of, and if there be any dispute as to the reasonableness or otherwise of the price paid by him, such dispute shall be referred to arbitration as provided by Rule 13. The term "Full Grade" shall be understood to mean the difference between "fine" and "fully good" and other similar differences. If, however, when a lot of cotton is tendered before the due date of the contract, the quality of the cotton should be objected to by the buyer, the seller shall be allowed to withdraw the tender and make a new tender within the contract time, provided no arbitration has been held on the cotton; but no withdrawal of any tender shall be allowed after an arbitration has been held.

Exception (*a*) Where the difference between the market rates for the grade contracted for, and for the full grade next below exceeds Rs. 10, the cotton must be taken by the buyer unless more than half grade off.

(23) In case either party shall be dissatisfied with the award under Rule 18, a right of appeal shall lie to the Appeal Committee, provided it be claimed before 1 p.m. (Standard Time) on the day, after the day on which the arbitration has been held, and provided also that the appellant pays the usual appeal fee of Rs. 50, and an award made and signed by at least three members of the Appeal Committee and countersigned by the Secretary shall be deemed to be the award of the Appeal Committee and shall in all cases be final.

(24) In cases where the buyer elects to reject, notice in writing to that effect shall be given to the seller and original tenderer not later than 1 p.m. (Standard Time) on the day, after the day on which the arbitration has been held, and the seller in such cases shall have the right to appeal up to 3 p.m. (Standard Time) on the same day, and the contract or contracts or the subject-matter of the contract should be lodged with the Secretary for the guidance of the Appeal Committee.

(*a*) In cases where the buyer elects to reject (after an appeal), notice in writing to that effect shall be given to the seller and the original tenderer not later than 1 p.m. (Standard Time) on the day following that on which the appeal is finally disposed of.

(25) The buyer shall in all cases begin to take delivery of the cotton not later than the day after the cotton is finally approved of, and shall continue to do so at the rate of not less than 300 bales per day. In default the seller may, after 48 hours' notice, weigh over the cotton at the expense and risk of the buyer, who shall then pay for it with interest at 9 per cent. per annum and 8 annas a bale for charges, failing which the seller shall have the power of re-sale for account and risk of the buyer. The seller shall not be held responsible for damage by rain water caused after the approval of the cotton if the same be not weighed over within 72 hours after final approval.

(26) The last buyer must pay for the cotton at the rate at which the Delivery Order was originally issued, and for the actual weight delivered; but for the purposes of settlement and for the adjustment of accounts between intermediate parties on Delivery Orders passed on, the weight of all bales referred to in these Rules shall be considered to be 3½ cwts. *net* per bale, and the sums due on such settlements and adjustment of accounts shall become payable when the cotton is finally passed.

Any settlement or adjustment of accounts under this Rule shall not be deemed to prejudice any other right which parties may have in respect of their contracts.

(27) In contracts for full-pressed bales, the buyers shall have the option of rejecting burst or re-pressed bales over 2 per cent. beyond those opened for inspection or arbitration. But the term " re-pressed " shall not be held to include bales which have only had the centre hoops refixed.

(28) When the due date falls on Sunday or on the following holidays, *viz.*, Good Friday, Christmas Day, New Year's Day, and the day fixed by the Governor-General in Council for the observance of the King's Birthday in India, it shall be considered as falling on the previous day; nor shall Sunday or any of the days as mentioned above be computed as forming any portion of the time allowed for any purpose under these Rules.

The Directors may, at their discretion, by a resolution passed by the Board of Directors of the Association, close the room of the Association at Colaba, on any day or days other than those above-mentioned, but any day or days on which the rooms are so closed as aforesaid, shall not affect the due date of contracts nor the time in which notice for " Appeal " or " Rejection " must be given under Rules 23, 24 and 24 (a), but such day or days on which the rooms are so closed as aforesaid, shall not be computed in the time allowed for arbitration under Rule 18.

(29) For the purposes of these Rules the expression " the market rate of the day " shall be taken to mean the rate quoted by the Daily Quotation Committee of the Association, subject to the right of

Appeal to the Board of Directors on payment of the usual Appeal fee of Rs. 50 or in the absence of any such quotation that quoted by the Board of Directors.

(30) The Official Quotations issued by the Bombay Cotton Trade Association, Limited, are " Jaitha Terms," *i.e.,* inclusive of 8 annas per bale muccadum allowance for all descriptions of cotton excepting Bengals and Sind for which descriptions the rates quoted for " Delivery Contracts " are " Railway Terms " and for " Ready purchases " " Jaith Terms."

(31) Claims for excess measurement for all descriptions of cotton must be sent in not later than six weeks after the complete lot has been received by the buyer.

(32) For the purpose of enforcing any award by attachment or otherwise, these rules and any contract referring thereto and the memorandum of the appointment of the arbitrators, may be made a rule of the High Court of Judicature of Bombay.

(33) The foregoing rules shall be applicable to all contracts made under the Rules and Regulations of this Association on and after 1st May, 1911.

Note.—At an Extraordinary General Meeting of the Shareholders, held on 27th May, 1909, it was resolved that the Contract Form (copy of which will be found on p. 108) be adopted and recognised as the Official Contract Form of the Bombay Cotton Trade Association, Limited

Form of Notice recommended to be used under Rule 22.

Sir,

I beg to give you notice that I refuse to take the cotton tendered by you in fulfilment of the contract of which particulars are given below under the provisions of Rule 22 of the Bombay Cotton Trade Association Rules.

Yours truly,

Dated ....

Particulars of Contract.

RULES REGARDING MEASURING COTTON AT JAITHAS AND/OR GODOWNS IN COLABA.

Members and Associate Members requiring bales of Bengal or Sind cotton measured at their Jaithas or Godowns at Colaba must send the fee and give notice in writing to the Secretary of the Bombay Cotton Trade Association, Limited, stating :—

1st.—Marks and number of bales.
2nd.—Where the bales are stored.
3rd.—The latest date on which they require the bales measured.

The Secretary of the Association, on receipt of the fee and application, will arrange with the Secretary of the Chamber of Commerce for a measurer to attend at the place named as soon as possible after receipt of the application.

The fee for measuring will be the usual one, *viz.*, 3 pies per bale of each lot for which the average measurement is certified.

At least 5 per cent. of each lot will be measured (the bales being selected by the measurer), and a certificate of the average measurement will be given to the applicant.

The rate of freight on which the claims for extra measurement are based will be fixed by the Directors at their monthly meetings, and will be applicable for all claims made during the following month on cotton measured in the Jaithas and/or Godowns under these Rules.

N.B.—The Secretary of the Chamber of Commerce hopes to be able to arrange for a measurer to attend on *the day after* the receipt of the application, but in order to facilitate the working of the scheme, firms are requested to give as long a notice as possible, and, when possible, to avoid asking for their bales to be measured at the end of the month, when the work of measuring bales at the Bunders and Docks is generally much heavier than it is early in the month.

(*Resolution adopted at Directors' Meeting held on 12th November, 1906.*)

Rule 26 of the Bombay Cotton Trade Association, Ltd., applies to adjustment of accounts between intermediate parties on Delivery Orders passed on, but does not apply to cases where Railway Receipts are passed on.

In cases where a Railway Receipt is passed on against a contract, Rule 26 does not apply, and as each seller receives·90 per cent. of his contract price in exchange for the Railway Receipt, there is only a small difference to adjust between intermediate parties and this must be settled on actual weight delivered.

In cases where a Delivery Order is passed on against a contract, Rule 26 applies, and the differences due between intermediate parties must, under this Rule, be settled on the basis of 3½ cwt. net per bale, and such differences become due when the cotton tendered has been finally passed.

Original.

OFFICIAL DELIVERY ORDER FORM OF THE

BOMBAY COTTON TRADE ASSOCIATION, LTD.

No........... *Bombay,*..................191 .

Time for Arbitration expires on..................................191 .

To

....

....

Please deliver to ....

.... Bales of .... Cotton

Sold as ....

as specified below, lying in ....

and take a receipt for the same.

Against Contract No. ...., dated ....

Mark.	Bales.	Price.	Terms.

Signature ....

10lbs. per 100 Bales allowed for Samples.

OFFICIAL DELIVERY ORDER FORM.

ENDORSEMENTS.

Please deliver to ....

Against Contract dated .... at Rs. ....,......... Terms.

Signature ....

Date ....

Please deliver to ....

Against Contract dated .... at Rs. ....,......... Terms.

Signature ....

Date ....

Please deliver to ....

Against Contract dated .... at Rs. ....,......... Terms.

Signature ....

Date ....

Please deliver to ....

Against Contract dated .... at Rs. ....,......... Terms

Signature ....

Date ....

Please deliver to ....

Against Contract dated .... at Rs. ....,......... Terms.

Signature ....

Date ....

No...............

MEMO. OF CONTRACT

From ....

To Messrs. ....

We have this day bought by your order and for your account subject to the rules and regulations of the Bombay Cotton Trade Association, Ltd.

From Messrs. ....

....(............) *Bales*

of .... *Cotton*

at Rs. ....*per Candy, less* 5¼% *Discount*

delivered in Bombay in full pressed bales.

Measurement..*tons per* 100 *Bales*

Delivery from...................*to*.........................*at seller's option.*

The quality to be..

Terms...

Remarks.

RULE 16, BOMBAY COTTON TRADE ASSOCIATION, LIMITED.

In every contract made under these rules the purchaser shall be deemed (subject to the provisions of Rule 22) to have agreed to accept in fulfilment of such contract any Cotton which may be passed either without an allowance or with an allowance awarded on arbitration or appeal under Rule 12.

Bombay, ...191 .

BROKERS.

Seller's Signature...

Official Contract Form of the Bombay Cotton Trade Association, Ltd.

No...............

MEMO. OF CONTRACT.

From..

To Messrs. ....

We have this day sold by your order and for your account subject to the rules and regulations of the Bombay Cotton Trade Association, Ltd.

To Messrs. ....

....(............) *Bales*

of .... *Cotton*

at Rs. ....*per Candy, less* 5¼% *Discount*

delivered in Bombay in full pressed bales.

Measurement..*tons per* 100 *Bales*

Delivered from...................*to*.........................*at seller's option.*

The quality to be..

Terms...

Brokerage ½% *to be paid by the seller.*

Remarks.

RULE 16, BOMBAY COTTON TRADE ASSOCIATION, LIMITED.

In every contract made under these rules the purchaser shall be deemed (subject to the provisions of Rule 22) to have agreed to accept in fulfilment of such contract any Cotton which may be passed either without an allowance or with an allowance awarded on arbitration or appeal under Rule 12.

Bombay, ...191 .

BROKERS.

Seller's Signature...

Buyer's Signature ....

Official Contract Form of the Bombay Cotton Trade Association, Ltd.

Table showing the Commercial Classification of the Principal Indian Cottons.

General name of the Growth.	Sub-divisions of the Growth according to — Province or District.	Station or Town.	Remarks.
Broach or Surtee-Broach.	Broach	Miagam and to the south about 7 others.	$\frac{7}{8}''$ to 1″ staple.
	Surat	Surat, Nausári and 19 others.	
Kumpta	South Bombay	Dhárwár. Gadag. Hubli.	$\frac{5}{8}''$ to $\frac{7}{8}''$ staple.
Saw-ginned Dhárwár.	Do.	Gadag. Hubli.	
Westerns ..	North Bombay ..	Annigeri, Bágalkot, Sholápur, Belgaum, Bijápur, Miraj and about 30 others.	
	Nizam's Dominion	Raichore and 5 others.	
	Madras	Bellary and 12 others.	
Dhollera ..	Cutch	About 10 towns.	
	Northern Gujarát.	About 20 towns.	
	Káthiáwár ..	Wadhwán, Bhávnagar, Junágad, Dhollera and about 40 others.	From many of these places a variety known as "Mathia" is also obtained which is distinguished thus :—"Bhávnagar (Mathia)."
Umras (or Umrawatti).	Beláti: Berar ..	Amráuati and 10 others.	Short stapled.
	Beláti: Central Provinces.	Nágpur, Pulgaon and 10 others.	
	Khándesh: Khándesh ..	Jalgaon, Dhulia and about 20 others.	Medium length.
	Khándesh: Central India	Indore and about 6 others.	
	Khándesh: Central Provinces.	Burhánpur. Harda. Khandwa.	
	Berar	Akola and 20 others	This is Umras proper and fairly long in staple.
	Hinganghát ..	Hinganghát and about 2 others.	Long staple.
	Bársi	Bársi and 10 others	
	Nagar	Ahmednagar and 10 others	

Table Showing the Commercial Classification of Cotton.

Bengals	Rájputána ..	Kekvi and 20 others.	Improving in quality.
	Central India ..	....	
	Bengal	Comilla	This is Bengal proper.
	United Provinces.	Cawnpore and about 20 others.	Short staple.
Sind, Punjâb ..	....	Over 30 stations in Sind and Punjab.	
Coconada ..	Madras	Coconada and Gantur.	
Tinnevelly ..	Do.	Coimbatore and about 12 others.	
Tinnevelly American, or Cambodia ..	Do.	South of Madras and Bombay Presidency.	1″ and more, long staple, heavy yielder; second "flush" inferior quality.

Final Estimate of the Cotton Crop of India (in thousands).

Provinces and States.	1911–12. Area (acres).	1911–12. Yield (bales).	1910–11. Area (acres).	1910–11. Yield (bales).	1909–10. Area (acres).	1909–10. Yield (bales).
Bombay (*a*)	4,668	556	6,528	1,316	5,794	1,426
Central Provinces and Berar	4,632	913	4,487	629	4,167	1,070
Madras (*a*)	2,149	250	1,873	235	1,569	180
Punjab (*a*)	1,584	241	1,385	306	1,436	396
United Provinces (*a*)	921	251	1,347	348	1,241	384
Sind (*a*)	330	120	279	97	214	104
Burma	183	34	167	28	198	32
Eastern Bengal and Assam	101	20	101	31	99	18
Bengal (*b*)	92	21	68	18	67	17
North-West Frontier	56	12	33	8	32	7
Ajmer-Merwara	25	11	45	20	39	13
Hyderabad	3,234	300	3,562	293	3,401	461
Central India	1,391	227	1,349	237	1,068	221
Barodo	665	96	806	134	675	235
Rajputana	(*c*) 263	(*c*) 73	465	143	464	148
Mysore	(*d*) 99	(*d*) 10	100	10	81	6
Total	20,363	3,135	22,595	3,853	20,545	4,718

N.B.—A Bale contains 400 lbs. of cleaned cotton.

(*a*) Including Native States within provincial boundaries. (*b*) Excluding Native States for which the yield is roughly estimated at 1,000 bales. (*c*) For certain States figures reported in the December forecast have been taken to make up the total, as final reports from those States have not been received. (*d*) Taken from the December forecast as final report has not been received. Final report just received gives 101,000 acres and 17,000 bales.

GLOSSARY OF WORDS.

Abkalani - - Inundation.
Bania - - - The shop-keeping Hindu, who is usually a moneylender.
Barani cultivation- Cultivation on rain water only.
Beegah - - Land measure of half an acre.
Berseem - - Egyptian clover.
Bosi Crop - - A crop grown on land previously flooded from a canal.
Bund - - - Embankment (generally applied to river embankments).
Charki cultivation- Cultivation irrigated by lifting water on to the land.
Cusecs - - - Cubic feet per second in irrigation.
Dubari - - - A second crop grown on the strength of the first crop's watering—not to be confused with watered dubari.
Fakir - - - Religious mendicant.
Gur - - - Raw sugar.
Hari - - - Cultivator.
Jagir land - - Land granted revenue free, either in perpetuity ("pusht be pusht") or resumable in whole or in part on the death of the guarantees.
Jagirdar - - Holder of Jagir land.
Kacha - - - Land thrown up by river silt, unsettled, temporary.
Kalar land - - Land impregnated with salts.
Kharif season - Inundation or flood season, taken as April to September in the Punjab and in Sind.
Khoso pani - - "Sour" water run off from rice fields to allow of fresh water taking its place.
Lakh or Lac - - One hundred thousand.
Malkano - - The payment made to Government on new land for the right of occupation.
Moke cultivation - Cultivation by flow from canals.
Muccadam - - Head man of a gang of labourers.
Pír - - - Mohammedan Priest—a hereditary title.
Rabi season - - The season when the river is low, taken as October to March in the Punjab and in Sind.
Ran - - - Desert.
Ryat - - - A peasant farmer.
Sailabi cultivation- Cultivation on land which has been flooded from the river.
Takavi - - - Advances made to cultivators by their landlords, and by Government to their tenants, for the purchase of seed, or for improving their canals.
Taluka - - - Revenue subdivision of a district.
Wah - - - Canal.
Zemindar - - Landowner.

TABLE OF WEIGHTS.

The Weights used in the various Provinces are very different The following tables have been taken from a compilation issued by Mr. Kuvarji Ardesir Makidalal:

KHANDESH.

80 Tolas = 1 Seer.
40 Seers = 1 Maund = $82 \cdot \frac{2}{7}$lbs.*
3 Maunds = 1 Pukka = 246·91lbs.*
*1lb. = 38·88 Tolas. 1 Seer = $2\frac{2}{5}$lbs.

Throughout the whole district same weight is obtainable, and cotton is sold by the rate per Pulla.

BERAR.

28lbs. = Maund.
10 Maunds = Boja.

Throughout the district same weights are used, and cotton is sold by rate per Boja of 10 Maunds or Quarters.

CENTRAL PROVINCES

80 Tolas = 1 Seer.

Pulgaon and Wardha.
11 Seers = 1 Maund = $22\frac{9}{16}$lbs.
15 Maunds = 1 Boja = $12\frac{1}{8}$ Quarters.

Nagpore and Sindhi.
12 Seers = 1 Maund.
14 Maunds = 1 Boja.

Cotton is sold by rate per Boja in the whole district.

BARSI AND NAGAR.

80 Tolas = 1 Seer.
40 Seers = 1 Maund.
3 Maunds = 1 Pulla.

One Boja of cotton weighs about one Pulla, and a Boja contains 2 Dhocras.

BARSI (NIZAM'S DOMINIONS).

80 Tolas = 1 Seer.
12 Seers = 1 Maund.
$10\frac{1}{2}$ Maunds = 1 Boja = $259\frac{1}{4}$lbs.

KARNATAK (KUMPTA).

Bijapore.
25lbs. = 1 Maund.
8 Maunds = 1 Atki = 200lbs.

Bhagalkote.
25lbs. = 1 Maund.
12 Maunds = 1 Barmani = 300lbs.

Dharwar, Gadag, and Hubli.
28lbs. = 1 Maund (1 Quarter).
12 Maunds = 1 Barmani = 336lbs.

THE WESTERNS.

25lbs. = Maund.
12 Maunds = 1 Barmani Boja.

SURAT.

37·03 Tolas = 1 Seer.
40 Seers = 1 Maund.
21 Maunds = 1 Candy = 800lbs.

Cotton sold by Candies.

BROACH.

40 Tolas or 41 Rupees } = 1 Seer.
40 Seers = 1 Maund = $42\frac{1}{6}$lbs.
21 Maunds = 1 Candy = $885\frac{3}{4}$lbs.

KATHIWAR.

Wadhwan.

40 Tolas = 1 Seer.
40 Seers = 1 Maund = 41 15lbs.

Bhownagar and Dhulia.

40 Tolas = 1 Seer.
40 Seers = 1 Maund = $42\frac{1}{7}$lbs.
24 Maunds = 1 Candy = $1011\frac{3}{7}$lbs.

Amreli and other places.

25 Maunds = 1 Candy = $1028\frac{4}{7}$lbs.

BENGAL.

104lbs. = 1 Maund of Cotton.
$82\frac{2}{7}$lbs. = 1 Maund of Kapas.

Cotton sold by Maunds of 40 Seers or 104 lbs ∴ 1 Seer = 2·60lbs.

TINNEVELLY.

500lbs. = 1 Candy.
Cotton sold per Candy.

Taylor, Garnett, Evans & Co., Ltd.,
Manchester, Reddish,
and London.

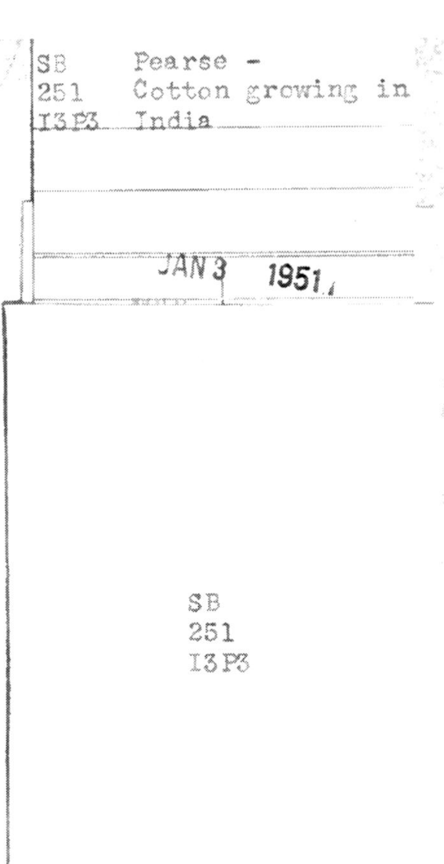

CPSIA information can be obtained at www.ICGtesting.com
Printed in the USA
LVOW10s2138080816

499569LV00015B/257/P